Tetrabiblos for the 21st Century

Ptolemy's Bible of Astrology, Simplified

Claudius Ptolemy

Translated by Sylvia Sky

Copyright 2023 by Catherine Rankovic

Sylviasky.com

No part of this book may be reproduced or transcribed in any form or by any means, electronic or mechanical, including photocopying or recording or by any information storage and retrieval system without written permission from the author and publisher, except in the case of brief quotations embodied in critical reviews and articles. Requests and inquiries may be mailed to: American Federation of Astrologers, Inc., 6535 S. Rural Road, Tempe, AZ 85283.

ISBN-13: 978-0-86690-685-2

Cover Design: Sylvia Sky

Back cover: Valery Brozhinsky/Shutterstock.com

Published by:
American Federation of Astrologers, Inc.
6535 S. Rural Road
Tempe, AZ 85283

Preface

Ptolemy's ancient all-in-one astrology manual is called *Tetrabiblos* because it has "four books" or sections, and astrologers have long called it "the bible of astrology." Claudius Ptolemy of Egypt wrote it late in his life, about 150 years after Christ, compiling and organizing what his ancient world knew about predictive astrology—an art and science that might have been lost to us except that handwritten copies of *Tetrabiblos* survived in Greek, Arabic, and Latin, because even when astrology was forbidden there were always those who against the rules could appreciate it.

Ptolemy was an astronomer and astrologer when those disciplines were one. From his many other books we know he was above all a scientist and mathematician who believed in logic and order, and he saw—he *proved*—the mathematical basis of planetary motion. *Tetrabiblos* combines science and art to explain how stars and planets yield meaning. This book laid the foundation for Western astrology as it is practiced today.

Astrologers of Ptolemy's time had seven planets to work with; the 21st century began with ten planets in our solar system and might end with many more. Earth was at the center of Ptolemy's universe, with the "spheres" of the Moon, Sun and planets encasing it, and although that view is outmoded, astrology still operates on a geocentric basis. Ptolemy singled out the Sun and Moon as the most important planets, and astrologers today do the same. Although he gave more weight to planets than to signs, the zodiac then had the 12 signs familiar to us today, and his horoscope charts had 12 houses, all with the meanings they have now. He defined the five major planetary aspects: the conjunction, sextile, square, trine, and opposition. He emphasized the power of the four "angles" in a chart, meaning the ascendant, midheaven, descendant, and nadir. We do that, too. Astrologers no longer believe in killer planets or four terrestrial elements, nor do they characterize nations and races as Ptolemy did, sweepingly and in terms we of today might find offensive. But he is much, much braver about predictive astrology than astrologers are today, and that is the chief reason to read and learn from him.

Scholars who can read the original Greek admire Ptolemy as a mathematician and scientist, yet agree that he was not a good writer. In fact *Tetrabiblos* was such difficult reading that by the ninth century C.E. another writer had paraphrased the book to make it more readable. Preserved in an Arabic manuscript, this "Paraphrase of Proclus" is the oldest surviving version of *Tetrabiblos*. Compared with the full text, it cuts corners and contains inaccuracies. This new translation is the full text, adapted from the two most recent English translations, published in 1822 and 1940.

Tetrabiblos was first translated into English in 1701. By then, generations of copyists writing in Greek, Latin, and Arabic had handed down errors and ambiguities and inserted their own ideas and commentary into the text. Twentieth-century scholars compared the 35 or so most reliable manuscripts to come up with what they think is close to Ptolemy's original, which has not survived. They can identify Ptolemy's writing because he wrote ponderous prose: ponderous, but not pretentious.

His is the voice of an instructor and mentor. The final page of *Tetrabiblos* has always gone missing and for 2000 years people have tried to finish the book for him.

Because the currently available English translations are so dense and hard to read, few of today's Western astrologers have actually read their "bible of astrology," even as they follow thoroughly Ptolemaic instructions for casting and interpreting natal charts, and dole out astrological advice 99 percent derived from *Tetrabiblos*. I thought astrology's basic reference book should be widely available in a version simpler to read and use.

So using as my primary source the definitive and doggedly word-for-word 1940 English translation by F.E. Robbins, with J.M. Ashmand's 1822 *Paraphrase of Proclus* translation as a backup, I reworded *Tetrabiblos* into contemporary English. Ptolemy called planets "stars," and sometimes called ascendant points "horoscopes"; I call them what astrologers call them now. Where translations said "maleficent" I wrote "unfavorable," and where they said "quartile" I wrote "square." Ptolemy does not use the word "decans" to describe ten-degree fractions of signs and houses, but when that's what he clearly meant, I used it. Rather than a word-for-word translation, because we have that, I wanted clarity and to define terms and concepts when necessary, to encourage its use as the reference book it was intended to be. Bullet points and lists reinforce the text and in a few places I inserted examples to illustrate concepts otherwise hard to grasp.

Certain points in the text have been arguable for centuries. Settle those arguments I cannot. Nor do I wish to litigate the finer points of Hellenistic astrology or Koine Greek. I simply wanted to read *Tetrabiblos* and discovered that after reading every quaint or tortuous paragraph I had to write my own paragraph re-stating in plain English what I'd just read, and then re-read the passage to confirm I had grasped what it said, then correct my plain-English paragraph, and so on. No one else should have to do that.

Although called a "bible," *Tetrabiblos* is not gospel. Even Ptolemy says that astrology cannot tell us everything and predictions can be wrong. Some of his statements are overspecific, outmoded, opinionated, outlandish, or by our standards offensive, but I did not censor or sweeten them. Compared to our world, Ptolemy lived in a very small one, and thought his own location, Alexandria, Egypt, was its hub and the home of the best people. I made a good-faith effort in Book Two to provide the modern names of ancient nations and regions. The chapters in Book Three about predicting the length of a life are a swamp of famously terrible prose in which Ptolemy was perhaps trying to camouflage his doubts or lack of clarity. My overall goal was an English-language "translation" more readable, accurate, and useful than the *Paraphrase of Proclus* provides.

Ptolemy wrote his book when astrology was all about predictions. *Tetrabiblos* can strengthen our confidence in astrology's predictive capabilities. I hope those like myself who have struggled to read *Tetrabiblos* and people interested in the fundamentals of Western astrology can now access what the world's most important astrologer said.

Sylvia Sky, 2018

Contents

Book One

1.1. Is Prediction Possible?	3
1.2. What Astrology Can Tell Us, and What It Can't	3
1.3. Astrology is Useful	6
1.4. The Powers of the Planets (including the Sun and Moon)	8
1.5. Favorable and Unfavorable Planets	9
1.6. Planets Masculine and Feminine, Eastern or Western	10
1.7. Daytime and Nighttime Sects and Planets	10
1.8. Moon Phases and Planetary Retrogrades	11
1.9. Fixed Stars and Their Ruling Planets	11
1.10. The Four Seasons, Four Winds, and Four Cardinal Points or Angles	15
1.11. The Types of Zodiac Signs	16
1.12. About Masculine and Feminine Signs	17
1.13. The Aspects: Conjunction, Sextile, Square, Trine and Opposition	18
1.14. Some Signs Command and Others Obey	19
1.15. Signs and Degrees that "Behold" or "Mirror"	20
1.16. Disjunct Signs	20
1.17. Planetary "Lords" or Rulers	20
1.18. Zodiac Signs that Harmonize: Triplicities	21
1.19. Exalted and Fallen Planets	22
1.20. Subdividing the Signs the Egyptian Way	24
1.21. Subdividing the Signs the Chaldean and Ptolemaic Ways	25

1.22. Overthinking Places and Degrees	26
1.23. Faces, Chariots, and Other Beliefs	26
1.24. What the Spaces Between the Planets Mean	27

Book Two

2.1. Introduction	31
2.2. How People Are Shaped by Their Environments	31
2.3. Nations, Their Triplicities, and Their Traits	32
Europe	32
Eastern Ethiopia or South Asia	33
Northeast Asia	34
Libya	35
Where the Quarters Meet	36
Quick Reference List	36
2.4. Making General Predictions from Eclipses	37
2.5. Where Will the Eclipse Have Its Greatest Impact?	37
2.6. Timing the Predicted Events	37
2.7. Who or What Will Be Affected?	38
2.8. The Quality and Nature of the Effect	40
2.9. Of the Colors of Eclipses, Comets, and Similar Phenomena	42
2.10. About the New Moon of the Year	42
2.11. How the Signs and Their Decans Affect the Weather	43
2.12. Investigating the Weather in Detail	45
2.13. About Daily and Minor Atmospheric Phenomena	46

Book Three

3.1. What We Are Born With	50
3.2. Pinpointing the Ascendant	51

3.3. Questions a Natal Horoscope Can Answer	52
3.4. About the Parents and Planetary "Attendants"	55
3.5. About Brothers and Sisters	57
3.6. Predicting a Baby's Gender	58
3.7. Predicting Twins or Multiple Births	58
3.8. Birth Defects	59
3.9. Babies That Die, are Given Up, or Abandoned	60
3.10. Figuring the Potential Lifespan	60
3.11. An Example of Lifespan Calculation	65
3.12. Looks and Temperament	66
3.13. About Sicknesses and Injuries	68
3.14. The Quality of the Character	70
3.15. Of Diseases of the Soul	75

Book Four

4.1. What Life Will Bring	78
4.2. About Riches	78
4.3. Will Life Be Happy?	79
4.4. Which Occupation?	79
4.5. About Marriage and Love	82
4.6. Having Children	84
4.7. About Friends and Enemies	85
4.8. Travel Abroad	87
4.9. The Quality of Death	88
4.10. About the Ages of Man	90
4.11. Predictions Using Primary Directions	91
Index	95

Tetrabiblos

Book One

1.1. Is Prediction Possible?

1.2. What Astrology Can Tell Us, and What It Can't

1.3. Astrology is Useful

1.4. The Powers of the Planets (including the Sun and Moon)

1.5. Favorable and Unfavorable Planets

1.6. Planets Masculine and Feminine, Eastern or Western

1.7. Daytime and Nighttime Sects and Planets

1.8. Moon Phases and Planetary Retrogrades

1.9. Fixed Stars and Their Ruling Planets

1.10. The Four Seasons, Four Winds, and Four Cardinal Points or Angles

1.11. The Types of Zodiac Signs

1.12. About Masculine and Feminine Signs

1.13. The Aspects: Conjunction, Sextile, Square, Trine and Opposition

1.14. Some Signs Command and Others Obey

1.15. Signs and Degrees that "Behold" or "Mirror"

1.16. Disjunct Signs

1.17. Planetary "Lords" or Rulers

1.18. Zodiac Signs that Harmonize: Triplicities

1.19. Exalted and Fallen Planets

1.20. Subdividing the Signs the Egyptian Way

1.21. Subdividing the Signs the Chaldean and Ptolemaic Ways

1.22. Overthinking Places and Degrees

1.23. Faces, Chariots, and Other Beliefs

1.24. What the Spaces Between the Planets Mean

1.1. Is Prediction Possible?

Dear Friend,

These are the two best methods for making astrological predictions:

1. The choicest method is the scientific method: understanding the Sun, Moon and planets and their astronomical and mathematical relationships to each other and to our Earth.

2. The second-best method is drawing upon our trove of traditional knowledge. Over thousands of years, astrologers have passed down to us their observations about how the Sun, Moon and planets and the relationships between them, called aspects, seem to affect earthly events. That information can be useful when those aspects re-occur, as of course they will.

In my previous book, *The Almagest*, I explained the first method. But combining the two methods delivers the best results. So this book explains the second method clearly, systematically, and in detail.

"Why is the second method not as good as the first?" you might ask.

The first method relies on the cosmic order and the motion of the stars and planets. They never deviate from that order. From that certainty comes the first method's higher level of predictive accuracy.

The second method draws parallels between planetary aspects and events on Earth. We do not have written records from all the astrologers who have observed and studied the effects of planetary aspects. Even if we did, human observations are not scientific or perfectly consistent. What we do have, and can use, are time-tested human observations passed down to us as traditional knowledge.

Enveloped in the cosmos as we are, we're still humans living in a material world. Both humans and this world are imperfect. So the second method is bound to be as imperfect as humanity itself. Our trove of traditional knowledge lacks the mathematical perfection of the astronomical order. But those who say tradition is useless are wrong.

Astrologers wanting to use this second predictive method must first acknowledge that on Earth no two moments can ever be precisely alike. Our modern world is not an exact copy of the ancient world. We can draw parallels between today's events and past events, but those events can never be identical. That, however, doesn't render the second method "useless" for predicting the future.

But let's first discuss whether predicting the future is truly possible.

1.2. What Astrology Can Tell Us, and What It Can't

Our Earth is surrounded by an invisible, cloudlike atmosphere called "ether," and this ether permeates all earthly things. Ether drives fire and air; fire and air in turn drive earth and water. Those elements, in turn, drive life on Earth.

Fire, earth, air, and water are the four elements we on Earth know best, but ether is the fifth element and the greatest. Ether can interact with, and alter, animals and plants and all living things.

The Sun, acting as part of this cosmic ambience, affects Earth as a whole. Depending on the season, our Sun furnishes us with heat, moisture, dryness, or cold. The position of the Sun at midday defines our seasons. Under its influence, rivers will flow and animals will breed, and crops can be seeded and ripen. The Sun dominates all life. Yet the Sun's power can increase or decrease under planetary influences.

The Moon, our closest planetary neighbor, also has power over our Earth. Tides, rivers, plants, and animal life all wax and wane in synchrony with the Moon's cycle of waxing and waning. The Moon is most influential at the times of the new Moon, full Moon, and first and last quarters.

The constellations and their stars, which rise and set, and the planets that seem to wander through them also affect our earthly ambience, causing hot, windy, or stormy weather, conditions that certainly affect us all. Each planet and star, including the Sun and Moon, has its own character, and they all influence each other. Mercury, Venus, Mars, Jupiter and Saturn and particular fixed stars can be hard to see or pinpoint, and their effects on our lives are less obvious. But anyone can witness the Sun and Moon performing their every function beautifully, and see that together the Sun and Moon govern all earthly life cycles.

We on Earth are dependent on these greater forces, and the Sun's and Moon's positions in the heavens matter very much. Farmers will tell you that some times are better than others for planting seeds or breeding livestock. Even animals seem to know these things by instinct.

The best times, of course, are those that deliver the best results: the hardiest plants, or the sturdiest calves or lambs. Under lesser conditions, the results will not be as good. Therefore we can say that whatever grows has the qualities of its beginnings.

Generations of farmers have observed that the most favorable times to plant are when the Sun and Moon are positioned just so. They know well that life depends on these greater forces. Sailors and navigators know that, too. Tell farmers or sailors that the Sun's and Moon's positions in the sky are meaningless and have nothing to do with their lives, and they will think you are terribly ignorant.

Favorable Sun and Moon positions are not a guarantee that a beginning will blossom into a desired result, but through observation people have learned enough to bet their livelihoods on it.

Their forecasting could be even better if they'd been educated in astronomy, tracked the movements of the planets and were aware of each individual planet's nature and effects, and could measure and calculate all kinds of astronomical data. A person who did those things would have a greater chance of correctly predicting a distinct outcome.

If it is true that whatever grows has the qualities of its beginnings, by studying and interpreting the cosmic conditions or "ambience" at the time of a man's birth we can predict with a degree of confidence his physical, mental, and spiritual traits and capacities. We could predict that in adulthood he would prosper or might instead be unlucky or accident-prone.

Critics of astrology say predicting such things is impossible. Jeering when astrologers make predictions that turn out to be wrong, they declare astrology does not work. When astrology actually does seem to work, the same people say it was by chance. So any way they look at it, they can demean the whole science of astrology.

It is true that some astrologers do not know astrology as well as they should, and therefore their predictions are wrong. Blame the astrologer, then, or blame his teacher, but don't blame astrology itself. Then there are those fakes very good at fooling people and selling them "secrets" and "lucky numbers" and so on, calling themselves astrologers when they are not. But that's not astrology's fault either. We might as well say philosophy ought to be abolished because some people pretend to be philosophers.

Astrologers can and do make honest mistakes. That is simply because astrology is such a vast field of knowledge, and so great an art, that human beings, even honorable and professional astrologers, sometimes aren't a match for it.

Let me also point out to the skeptics and critics that the educated guess, or conjecture, is a factor in every profession. The doctor guesses at a diagnosis. It's an educated guess, but it's still a guess. The merchant guesses how much demand there might be for his goods. Sometimes they're wrong. The same with astrologers.

Reading the cosmos correctly involves many factors and requires so much attention to detail that we should be glad there is a "second-best" predictive technique to strengthen our astrological readings. Through observation the ancient astrologers learned that particular Sun and Moon positions, or certain stars rising, foretold or paralleled certain kinds of events on Earth. In our day, observing similar aspects, we are able to predict similar events. Yet because our world is not their world we might also make a wrong call.

Let me say again: Individual planetary aspects can and do repeat themselves, and that's a scientific fact, but conditions on Earth and in the rest of the heavens (and that includes all the stars and planets) will never be precisely the same as when the universe was born, or at any other time.

Unlike farmers and sailors who live by the weather, windy or snowy conditions when a person was born do not matter to the astrologer. Astrology concerns itself with not the earthly but the cosmic ambience of a birth: Sun, Moon, stars and planets. Yet I do have to say that individuals can't help but be affected by the earthly place and time they were born into. Nationality makes a difference, as do the local customs and culture.

A person's natal horoscope chart shows the cosmic ambience at the time of birth, but do understand that a horoscope alone will not tell us everything. A newborn's earthly environment will impart its influence. A doctor will consider not only the body his patient was born with but also the effects of his patient's background, upbringing, and locale on the patient's health and potential recovery. It's essential for an astrologer to do likewise.

The very important point I'm making here is that an astrologer using only a birth chart cannot explain or predict absolutely everything about a life. Some factors are outside a chart's jurisdiction. So that's another reason astrologers are sometimes mistaken.

Yes, the stakes are very high for those who try to predict the future. Astrologers are reaching toward the divine. If we manage to grasp even a handful of valuable information we should be happy with that.

Astrologers are of course obliged to do their utmost to compile from their information an accurate forecast. But please know that not every question has an answer or a complete answer, as much as we wish it did. Astrology is a great art and a beautiful science we should appreciate even when we can't squeeze from it every little detail we'd like to know.

1.3. Astrology Is Useful

So I've briefly shown that it is possible to predict conditions and events by watching and interpreting cosmic activity. In fact some people do it daily and thrive by it—without being astrologers.

Because all things have the qualities of their beginnings, a birth or natal horoscope can reveal the traits of a person's body and soul. The bodily traits include his temperament, his intellectual capacity, his physical appearance, whether he will be healthy or sickly, and how long he might live. The soul he was born with determines, among other things, whether or not he will prosper, marry, or have an honorable moral character. So with all these together we can foretell some of the events in his life.

Yes, we can actually do that, and it's very exciting. But when you, the astrologer, deliver an astrological opinion or forecast you must be able to give, seriously and in full, the reasoning behind everything you say (stifle your vanity and your imagination!). The information in this book will provide what you will need for serious forecasting.

Predictive astrology requires thought and precision. Don't be hasty or take it lightly. When you see in a chart a force that looks as if it will overwhelm all the opposing factors, say nothing until you have identified and weighed all the opposing and mitigating factors very, very carefully. Carelessness about this causes many failed predictions.

Astrology isn't infallible, but even so, it's worthwhile and it's useful.

Some people ask how astrological predictions could ever be useful. I say: What could be better, healthier, and more gratifying for the soul than allowing astrology to provide us with the fullest possible view of things human and divine? A man who knows the gifts he was born with can develop those gifts. Of course he'd like his horoscope to predict or ensure him riches and fame, but if that doesn't happen—well, philosophy has no power to make people rich and famous either, and we don't call that one of philosophy's failings. There's no justification for condemning either philosophy or astrology, although it's clear, or it should be clear, that astrology happens to offer more advantages.

Quite a few people think that astrological forecasts, correct or not, are useless. They're usually the type who don't care about important matters in general. They say events unfold regardless of predictions, so what's the use of knowing about them ahead of time?

Forecasting definitely has its uses. First, if we knew in advance what might happen, we wouldn't panic when meeting with what others call "the unexpected." Knowing the future, having "seen" it more or less, we'd be prepared to face calmly whatever came to us, or do what we could to avoid what's unfavorable.

Second, it's still news to some people that we can use astrology to actually avoid or sidestep some of our troubles. Many wrongly believe that one's natal horoscope determines one's fate at birth, sets it in stone, and all that will happen to them, good and bad, is cosmically pre-ordained and inevitable.

The only thing in the universe that is pre-ordained is the continual and orderly motion of the stars and planets. We human beings live on Earth with conditions we can change, or that nature can alter. Chance remains a factor in every earthly life. Situations evolve with and without our participation. When disasters such as epidemics or earthquakes overwhelm masses of people, it's not because these people's natal charts showed they all had it coming. Certain planetary transits unleash enormous, irresistible forces that will always overcome lesser forces. Understand it this way: During an earthquake or volcanic eruption, the fact that your natal horoscope says you are sexy and a money magnet is pretty much overwhelmed by circumstances.

Fortunately for all of us, such disasters are rare. Life's lesser troubles are more easily averted. Life will include accidents or mishaps simply because we live with nature. Sit on a hornet's nest and you will be stung—regardless of what's in your natal chart. Swim out beyond the limits of your strength and you will drown, regardless of what your natal chart might have said about your lifespan. Plants and animals and even rock formations give way to natural forces if nothing else intervenes.

So please don't believe in or promote the false impression that astrology can help a person avoid every accident or mishap. We all live with nature's forces, and Mother Nature isn't obliged to treat you differently because you have certain indicators in your horoscope.

Although astrology does not allow us to dodge every possible difficulty, predictive astrology can help us better manage some of them. Like a physician, an astrologer should be able to diagnose a problem and decide whether it's treatable or not. Without treatment, an illness will take its natural course, but when treatments and remedies are available they can reduce its severity even if they can't deliver a total cure.

I've also learned that the more specific and detailed a prediction is, the less likely it is that people will believe it. It's rare to find someone open-minded enough to give a detailed prediction a fair hearing.

The close-minded people who claim they don't believe in astrology still really believe, but they believe selectively. For example, most people will confidently predict, from their awareness of the Sun and Moon, that the coming year will have a springtime. They will also predict a summer, autumn, and winter because it's happened before. They can then plan how to live comfortably in each season.

Nobody thinks planning ahead for the coming season is odd. Yet if an astrologer is a bit more specific and predicts that the coming summer will be exceptionally warm, people will shrug and say that's only a guess.

They say this because they are unfamiliar with how real astrology works. It's a rare person who appreciates how much precision and care go into (or ought to go into) a specific prediction like that one.

People also think predictions are "all or nothing." Because they have not heard that some happenings are outside of astrology's control, if a prediction is not spot-on they will not give it credit for being partially correct. Even then it could benefit them, if only a little, by encouraging them to prepare.

The more deeply a person understands astrology, the more deeply he or she treasures astrological predictions, even when the benefits might be limited or predictions can't avert every problem.

And, very important: Too many people don't believe that we all can, to some extent, create our own futures. We can. The Egyptians developed advanced medical astrology because they understood that the future could be altered by their taking action now. Perhaps what the Egyptians practice should not be called "medical astrology" but instead "astrological medicine," because the first thing their doctors ask for when treating a sick individual is his or her natal horoscope. They think medical treatments ought to be customized for the individual, and by assessing an individual's horoscope they can prescribe the most likely cure. They do not wait for nature to take its course; when illness threatens, they use astrology to prevent or alleviate it as much as they can.

Now that we have finished this preliminary discussion, I will introduce and discuss the heavenly bodies one by one, and their powers and character, and what astrological tradition has discerned about them. At the top of our list, as they should be, are the powers of the Sun and the Moon and the planets.

1.4. About the Powers of the Planets (including the Sun and Moon)

Any heavenly body will have or encourage one or more of these four traits: hot, cold, moist, and dry. These four traits together we call the "the humours." Of the four, heat and moisture are considered "active," because in their presence all things increase. Coldness and dryness cause things to shrink or withdraw; these traits are called "passive."

The Sun

The Sun's essential nature and its tasks are heat and heating, and, to a lesser extent, drying or dehydrating. Its seasonal changes are easily seen and experienced. Whatever the season, when the Sun is at its zenith it provides the most heat we will have all day.

The Moon

The Moon does the opposite of the Sun: It hydrates. That's because it's close to the Earth and the Earth exhales moisture-rich vapors. Because the Moon reflects the Sun's light, the Moon does have some modest heating power, but mostly the Moon's influence softens and hydrates things, sometimes encouraging rot.

Saturn

We begin our list of the planets beyond the Sun and Moon with the one farthest from the Earth: Saturn. Saturn's natural quality is cooling. It has only modest drying capabilities because of its distance from the Sun, and Earth's moist exhalations can't reach it. But remember that any planet's aspects to the Sun and Moon can modify that planet's natural qualities, and so it is with Saturn.

Mars

The nature of the planet Mars is to dehydrate and to burn, because it's fiery red and nearer to the Sun.

Jupiter

Jupiter is temperate because this planet's sphere happens to be between the spheres of frigid Saturn and hot, burning Mars. It tends to be warm and moist rather than cold and dry. A good example of Jupiter's influence is the moist springtime wind that wakes the Earth and warms the soil.

Venus

Venus, like Jupiter, is temperate. Because it's close to the Sun, it does have mild heating powers, but it moistens like the Moon, because like the Moon it shines brightly and is close to the Earth's moist exhalations.

Mercury

Mercury's influence is sometimes dry and sometimes hydrating, and its influence quickly bounces between these extremes. It stays close to the hot Sun, yet has some qualities of the Moon.

1.5. Favorable and Unfavorable Planets

Because two of the "humours" are fertile and active (heat and wetness), and two are dehydrating and passive (cold and dryness), ancient astrologers accepted Jupiter, Venus, and the Moon as favorable planets because they had the favorable, creative traits of heat and wetness, although to different extents.

Faraway Saturn is very cold and dry, both destructive traits. Mars dries things out because Mars is excessively hot. So tradition has labeled these two planets as destructive and unfavorable.

The Sun and Mercury, however, can both generate heat and withdraw heat. They have this versatility in common. They can adapt and fuse their traits with those of the other planets, influencing a horoscope either favorably or unfavorably.

1.6. Planets "Masculine" and "Feminine," and Eastern or Western

In astrology, "masculine" and "feminine" are traits even more basic than our four "humors" of cold, dry, hot, and moist. Clearly, moistness is feminine. Tradition has therefore decreed that the Moon and Venus have "feminine" natures. All the others are masculine, except Mercury, which is some of both.

The ancients also assigned planets a gender depending on whether they appeared as morning stars or evening stars. They said morning stars, which are the planets which precede sunrise, are masculine; evening stars, which follow the setting Sun, are feminine. This is regardless of which planets they actually are.

The ancients even extended this idea, saying that all planets located from the eastern horizon to the midheaven—rising stars—and those which have set in the west and are approaching the nadir, are all masculine, and all the others feminine, again regardless of which planets they are. The ancients called the stars and planets in the east, or rising, "oriental," and stars and planets in the west "occidental." On a horoscope chart divided into quadrants and houses, the masculine quadrants are those containing houses 4, 5, and 6, and 10, 11, and 12.

There's also a school of thought that says any planet turns masculine or feminine when it travels through a "masculine" or "feminine" zodiac sign. The "masculine" zodiac signs are Aries, Gemini, Leo, Libra, Sagittarius and Aquarius. The "feminine" are Taurus, Cancer, Virgo, Scorpio, Capricorn, and Pisces.

1.7. Daytime and Nighttime Sects and Planets

Daytime is masculine because it's hot and active; nighttime is feminine because it's cool, receptive, and moist. Regardless of the time of day, every planet is designated either a daytime planet or a nighttime planet.

"Daytime" and "nighttime" are the two "sects."

Tradition says that the Moon and Venus, the cool planets, are always nighttime planets, and the Sun and Jupiter are always daytime planets. Mercury, with its dual nature, is again the exception: It's a daytime planet when it's a morning star, and a nighttime planet when it's an evening star.

Saturn and Mars, the planets with destructive tendencies, were assigned the daytime and the nighttime, respectively. These assignments were made with balance and proportion in mind: Placing Saturn in the daytime sect with the Sun and Jupiter moderates Saturn's typical dry chill, and Mars' dry heat is less extreme when in the company of the Moon and Venus.

Not only that, but when Saturn is brought into the "daytime" category its coolness helps balance the warm daytime planets, and Mars' heat balances the cold and wet "nighttime" sect with the nighttime planets Moon and Venus.

To summarize, the planets according to their "sects":

- Daytime Planets: Sun, Jupiter, Saturn
- Nighttime Planets: Moon, Venus, Mars
- Variable: Mercury

1.8. Moon Phases and Planetary Retrogrades

The Moon, Saturn, Jupiter, and Mars have greater or lesser powers depending on where they are in relation to the Sun. Let's start with the Moon:

From the new Moon to the first quarter, the Moon produces more moisture. From the first quarter to the full Moon, the Sun's increasing influence makes the Moon produce more heat. From full Moon to last quarter, the Sun influences the Moon toward dryness, and from last quarter to the new Moon, as its light diminishes, the Moon encourages cold.

The five planets, on a predictable schedule, at times can appear to halt in their paths across the sky and then move backwards. We call this backward motion "retrogradation" and speak of it saying "So-and-so planet is in retrograde." Retrograde motion is predictable and temporary.

When the planets start or finish their retrograde motion, they seem to slow down and then halt or stand still while they change direction. We then say these planets are "stationary" or "stationing." At the end of a retrograde period, the planet resumes "direct" or forward motion.

Planets rising in the east will encourage moisture when they halt or "station" and turn retrograde. When stationing they also encourage heat. The influence of retrograde planets can be enhanced or moderated by other planets.

1.9. Fixed Stars and Their Ruling Planets

The planets move against a backdrop of stars. Let's leave the planets for a moment to discuss these stars.

Stars in the night sky are called, by astrologers, "fixed stars," and each one has its own character traits.

Just as I've listed the traits of the planets, I will list the traits of the fixed stars, specifically those within the band of 12 constellations called the zodiac. As you probably know, each sign of the zodiac has as its constellation and symbol an animal, a being, or an object. To use the following information you should become familiar with the constellations.

Through observation we know that the fixed stars share traits with the planets. The fixed stars within the zodiac signs are our focus here.

Fixed Stars in Aries, the Ram

The stars in the head of Aries have an effect like the combined powers of Mars and Saturn. The stars in the jaw or mouth of Aries have powers like Mercury's and somewhat like Saturn's. The stars in the hind foot have the character of Mars, and those in the tail have Venus traits.

Fixed Stars in Taurus, the Bull

The constellation Taurus represents only the front half of a bull. Along the line where the front half ends are stars that have the temperature of Venus and a bit of Saturn. The stars in the cluster called the Pleiades have traits like those of the Moon and Jupiter. In the bull's head, among a star cluster called the Hyades, is one bright reddish star, nicknamed The Torch. This star, Aldebaran, has the temperature of Mars, and the others in the cluster have a temperature like Saturn's, with some Mercury blended in. The stars in the tips of the horns have Mars traits.

Fixed Stars in Gemini, the Twins

The stars of Gemini in the area we would call "the feet" of the twins have mainly the traits of Mercury, with some Venus. The bright stars in the thighs have Saturn's traits. Two bright stars mark the twins' heads. The one on the right, also called the Star of Apollo or Pollux, has Mercury's traits, and the one on the left has the traits of Mars, and is called the Star of Hercules, or Castor.

Fixed Stars in Cancer, the Crab

The two stars that represent the stellar crab's eyes have Mercury's traits, and some Mars traits. The stars in the claws have the traits of Saturn and Mercury. The cloud-like star cluster in the crab's chest, called the Beehive, has the traits of Mars and the Moon, and the two stars on either side of it, called the Donkeys, both have traits of Mars and the Sun.

Fixed Stars in Leo, the Lion

The two stars in the lion's head act as Saturn does, and, to a lesser degree, as Mars does. The three stars in the lion's throat also act mostly like Saturn, and secondarily like Mercury. The bright star in the lion's "heart," called Regulus, has Mars and Jupiter traits, and those in the lion's hip and the bright star in the tail have Saturn and Venus traits. The lion's thighs contain stars with the traits of Venus and, to a lesser degree, Mercury.

Fixed Stars in Virgo, the Virgin

The stars of Virgo are all influenced by Mercury. Those in the Virgin's head and the one on the tip of her southern wing have an effect mostly like Mercury but partly like Mars; the other bright stars in this wing and those of her belt again are like Mercury but tempered by Venus. The bright star in the northern wing, called Vindemiatrix, has Saturn's traits but some Mercury traits; and those in the tips of her feet and the train of her gown like that of Mercury and, to a lesser degree, Mars.

Fixed Stars in the Claws of the Scorpion

[*Ptolemy writes here as if the constellation Libra had not yet been established, although it had been established about 150 years previously. He uses here the constellation's old name, "Claws of the Scorpion," but uses "Libra" in the rest of the text.*] The two claws of the Scorpion, at their tips, have Jupiter and Mercury traits. In the middle, Saturn has the primary influence and Mars the secondary influence.

Fixed Stars in Scorpio, the Scorpion

The bright stars on the Scorpion's forehead act mostly like Mars and a bit like Saturn. The three in the Scorpion's body, including the red star Antares, act like Mars, but with a portion of Jupiter. The stars in the Scorpion's tail segments are like Saturn and, to some degree, Venus; those in the stinger, like Mercury and Mars. In the Scorpion's heart is a cloud-like star cluster, with influences like those of Mars and the Moon.

Fixed Stars in Sagittarius, the Archer

The point of the Archer's arrow acts like Mars and the Moon. Stars in his bow and his grip are like Jupiter and Mars. The cluster in his forehead is like the Sun and Mars; those in his cloak and his back, like Jupiter and, to a lesser degree, Mercury. Sagittarius has a horse's lower half, and the stars of his hooves are ruled by Jupiter and Saturn. The quadrangle on the tail has the influence of Venus, and to a lesser degree, Saturn.

Fixed Stars in Capricorn, the Sea-Goat

The stars in Capricorn's horns act mostly like Venus but a little like Mars; those in the mouth act as Saturn does, and to some degree, like Venus; those in the feet and belly, as Mars and Mercury; and those in the tail, Saturn and Jupiter.

Fixed Stars in Aquarius, the Water-Bearer

The shoulders of Aquarius have Saturn and Mercury traits, like those in the Water Bearer's left arm and cloak. The stars in his thighs are mostly like Mercury, with a bit of Saturn; and those in the stream of water pouring from his jar have traits like Saturn's and to some extent like Jupiter's.

Fixed Stars in Pisces, the Fishes

This constellation is divided into the Southern Fish and the Northern Fish, joined by a cord. The stars in the head of the Southern Fish act like Mercury and to some extent like Saturn; those in the Southern Fish's body like Jupiter and, secondarily, Mercury. Those in the tail and the southern cord are like Saturn, and then Mercury to a lesser extent. The Northern Fish's body and backbone stars are Jupiter's, with Venus secondarily. The northern part of the cord is Saturn and Jupiter together; and the bright star holding the cord together, Mars, and to some degree Mercury.

Stars in the Constellations North of the Zodiac

Here we will list constellations north of the zodiac, and their governing planets. The first planet listed is the primary influence; the second, when there is one, secondary:

- Ursa Minor: Saturn and Venus
- Ursa Major: Mars
- Coma Berenices: Moon and Venus
- Draco: Saturn, Mars and Jupiter

- Cepheus: Saturn and Jupiter
- Boötes: Mercury and Saturn; and its bright, tawny star Arcturus, Mars
- Corona: Venus and Mercury
- Hercules: Mercury
- Lyra: Venus and Mercury
- Cygnus: Venus and Mercury
- Cassiopeia: Saturn and Venus
- Perseus: Jupiter and Saturn, except in the star cluster in the hilt of his sword, which is Mars and Mercury.
- Auriga: Its brightest star Capella is influenced by Mars and Mercury.
- Ophiuchus: Saturn and Venus. The stars representing the serpent Ophiuchus is holding, Saturn and Mars.
- Sagitta [*"The Arrow," not the same as Sagittarius*]: Mars and Venus
- Aquila: Mars and Jupiter
- Delphinus: Saturn and Mars
- Pegasus: Mars and Mercury
- Andromeda: Venus
- Triangulum: Mercury

Stars in the Constellations South of the Zodiac

- The Southern Fish: Its bright star Fomalhaut: Venus and Mercury
- Cetus: Saturn
- Orion: The brightest stars in his shoulders are ruled by Mars and Mercury, and his other bright stars, Jupiter and Saturn.
- Eridanus: Jupiter and Saturn
- Lepus: Saturn and Mercury
- Canis Major: The bright star Sirius is ruled by Jupiter and Mars; its other stars, Venus.
- Canis Minor: The bright star Procyon is ruled by Mercury and Mars.
- Hydra: Its bright stars, Saturn and Venus
- Crater: Venus and Mercury
- Corvus: Mars and Saturn

- Argo: Its bright stars are influenced by Saturn and Jupiter.
- Centaurus: The stars in the human part of the centaur's body, Venus and Mercury, and in the equine part of the body, Venus and Jupiter
- Lupus: Saturn and Mars
- Ara: Venus and Mercury
- Corona Australis: Saturn and Mercury

The above are the traditional observations of the effects the fixed stars themselves have.

1.10. The Four Seasons, Four Winds, and Four Cardinal Points or Angles

The year has four seasons: spring, summer, autumn, and winter.

Spring is moist because it's between winter and summer, as Earth goes from cold to hot. Summer, when the Sun is highest, is hot and dry. Autumn is dryer, because summer's heat has depleted much of Earth's moisture. Winter is cold, with the Sun at its greatest distance away from the zenith and its arc low in the sky.

Technically, there is no real "beginning" to the zodiac because it's a circle, like a belt around the earth. But it was decided long ago, and it seems natural, that we use the spring or vernal equinox as the whole zodiac's starting-point. At that time the Sun is in Aries. So we take Aries as the zodiac's first sign.

The four seasons are like the four stages of life:

- At the spring equinox, all is moist and life is stirring. Because all youthful creatures are moist, and tender and delicate, we designate spring the first of the four seasons.
- The second stage is summer. We equate it with the prime of life, when heat rules.
- The third stage is autumn, when the year is past its prime, declining, and often drying or dried-out.
- The last stage is winter, and cold. This is the old age of our year.

[*Ptolemy writes from a northern-hemisphere perspective.*] There are four winds: east, south, west and north. They come to us from what we call the four cardinal points: east, south, west and north. Those directions and points have equivalents in a horoscope chart: the ascendant, midheaven, descendant, and nadir.

Each wind has unique qualities and effects, depending on the direction it comes from.

East. The east wind is likely to be dryest, because when the Sun is in the east, whatever has been moistened during the night begins drying up. We call this wind "Apeliotes," or "the wind that blows from the Sun." This eastern cardinal point is the same as the ascendant.

South. Our Earth, being on a tilted axis, offers more Sun to the countries south of us, and therefore they are hotter. The hot winds from the south we call "Notes." This southern cardinal point is the same as the midheaven.

West. As the Sun sets in the west and darkness comes, the things the Sun dehydrated during the day can grow moist again. So the winds from the west we call "Zephyrus": fresh, moist winds. This western cardinal point is the same as the descendant.

North. The winds of the north, where the Sun is low in the sky, are called "Bores." Their coldness causes things to condense and contract. This cardinal point is the same as the nadir.

We're mentioning these because variations in the seasons and winds cause variations in the influence of planets and stars. A planet designated "moist," or a star governed by a planet that is moist, will be at its most powerful when the winds and weather are moist. That same planet will have less influence, or a mixed influence, under hot and dry conditions.

1.11. The Types of Zodiac Signs

Now we'll discuss what tradition says about the qualities which are natural to the zodiac signs. For example, because the Sun passes through Aries, Taurus, and Gemini in the spring, those zodiac signs have spring-like qualities. That's generally true. But these signs also are affected by their relationships with the Sun, Moon, and planets.

So as not to get ahead of ourselves, let's lay a foundation by first discussing the powers of each zodiac sign as they would be if they were unrelated to all else in the heavens, and how they act upon each other.

Tradition says there are four kinds of zodiac signs: solstitial, equinoctial, solid or fixed, and mutable (also called bicorporeal) signs. Today we merge the first two kinds and say three kinds.

The Cardinal Signs

The spring equinox takes place when the Sun enters Aries, and the autumn equinox when the Sun enters Libra. Aries and Libra are the "equinoctial" zodiac signs. When the Sun is in these signs, the hours of daylight roughly equal the hours of darkness.

The summer solstice takes place when the Sun enters Cancer, and the winter solstice when the Sun enters Capricorn. Cancer and Capricorn are therefore the "solstitial" zodiac signs.

These above four zodiac signs, Aries, Cancer, Libra and Capricorn, are together called "cardinal" signs, "cardinal" in this case meaning "first," because they introduce the seasons.

The Solid or Fixed Signs

Four of the zodiac signs we call "fixed" or "solid" signs: Taurus, Leo, Scorpio, and Aquarius. These "solid" or "fixed" signs follow the cardinal signs in the usual zodiacal order.

When the Sun is in any of these "solid" signs, the current season is solidly established and in full swing. Humans experience at that time the purest expression of that season and have fully adapted to that season.

The Mutable or Bicorporeal Signs. Gemini, Virgo, Sagittarius, and Pisces are called "mutable" signs. When the Sun is in these signs, one season is ending and another starting; the weather is transitional. Traditionalists call these "bicorporeal" signs, "bicorporeal" meaning "two bodies."

For example, when the Sun is in Gemini, it's both late spring and early summer, so the zodiac sign Gemini has equally the traits of spring and summer. With the Sun in Virgo, summer is turning into autumn, so Virgo has both summer and autumn traits. With the Sun in Sagittarius, autumn is transitioning to winter; it has traits of both seasons. With the Sun in Pisces, winter is turning into spring; it has traits of two seasons. Thus these signs have two "bodies."

Here's that information in list form:

Cardinal Signs: Aries, Cancer, Libra, Capricorn

Fixed Signs: Taurus, Leo, Scorpio, Aquarius

Mutable or Bicorporeal Signs: Gemini, Virgo, Sagittarius, Pisces

1.12. About Masculine and Feminine Signs

Six signs are masculine and "diurnal" or daytime signs; six are feminine and nocturnal or nighttime signs. Masculine-feminine signs alternate all around the zodiac. Because Aries is the first zodiac sign, it's masculine, and masculine takes first place because its quality is active rather than passive, and active always trumps passive.

The spring equinox takes place when the Sun enters Aries. The autumn equinox happens when the Sun enters Libra, another masculine zodiac sign. Because of the equinoxes, these signs seem to have a special place and power in the universe, and therefore Aries and Libra are definitely designated masculine.

From Aries, we alternate masculine and feminine signs all the way through the zodiac, finishing with Pisces, a feminine sign.

Here's that information in list form:

- Aries: masculine
- Taurus: feminine
- Gemini: masculine
- Cancer: feminine
- Leo: masculine
- Virgo: feminine
- Libra: masculine
- Scorpio: feminine
- Sagittarius: masculine

Tetrabiblos

- Capricorn: feminine
- Aquarius: masculine
- Pisces: feminine

Some astrologers, however, believe that when casting a horoscope, the zodiac sign over the eastern horizon, no matter what zodiac sign it is, is masculine. That starts a chain of masculine-feminine-masculine-feminine all the way around the horoscope, so in that case, the usual masculine and feminine designations might be reversed. Those astrologers say they do this because the east, where the constellations rise, is the direction designated masculine.

We've already mentioned, in chapter 1.6, that some astrologers will say all signs from the eastern horizon to the midheaven are masculine, and all signs from the midheaven to the western horizon are feminine. Some astrologers divide the sky differently, and assign a gender to each section.

Astrologers also assign qualities to each zodiac sign depending on its shape: "Four-footed," "terrestrial," "commanding," and "fertile" are some of the labels used. Because the reasoning behind these labels seems obvious, we won't enumerate them all. If these signs happen to be prominent when we are making predictions, these labels can be useful.

1.13. The Aspects: Conjunction, Sextile, Square, Trine and Opposition

You've heard of planets in "conjunction," "opposition," or "square" to one another or in "trine" or "sextile" aspect to each other. These are the five aspects, or the five primary relationships the planets in a 360-degree horoscope chart might have to one another:

- Conjunction (planets, points or astral objects have exactly or close to 0 degrees between them)
- Sextile (approximately 60 degrees between them)
- Square (approximately 90 degrees between them)
- Trine (approximately 120 degrees between them)
- Opposition (approximately 180 degrees between them)

Every horoscope chart is a sky map, shaped like a circle. All the planets are somewhere within this circle. When we cast a horoscope for a certain day, time, and place, we create a map for the whole 360 degrees of that sky at that moment. In that map, we look at the positions of these planets and also their relationships to each other. Five of these relationships are the most significant, and here is what they mean:

A **"conjunction"** means that in a horoscope, planets occupy the same degree or very nearly. Planets in conjunction empower each other and enhance each other's strengths and weaknesses. Like a human couple they have their differences, but are a pair or a team. Most of the time this is a harmonious aspect. It is certainly a powerful one.

An **"opposition"** means that planets are 180 degrees apart, as far as possible from one another.

These planets in a horoscope act like enemies. Each wants the upper hand in the relationship. But there is something more than enmity involved because the two are still in a relationship. Two planets in opposition, like two human enemies, hope to undercut or at least neutralize the other's power. This aspect is not harmonious.

When two planets are 120 degrees apart, they are **"trine" or "in trine aspect"** to each other. The trine aspect is a harmonious aspect. The trine brings the planets involved into a pleasing relationship.

A **"square"** is two planets 90 degrees apart, or at a right angle to each other. This is a lesser version of an opposition. The two planets are like two people who challenge, annoy, and chafe one another. This aspect is not harmonious.

Two planets 60 degrees apart are **"sextile"** to one another [*"sextile" means "one-sixth"*]. They are kindly, helpful, and supportive, like ideal neighbors. This is a harmonious aspect.

Those are the five basic aspects that truly count in a horoscope. There are other aspects more obscure which we are not going to discuss.

The 360-degree circle of the horoscope chart is divided into 12 equal "houses" of 30 degrees each, one house per each sign of the zodiac. Every planet occupies one of those 12 houses, and each of those houses is governed by one of the 12 signs of the zodiac.

Remember, some of the signs are masculine and some feminine. The reason why conjunction, trine, and sextile aspects are called harmonious or favorable is because the signs bound together by those aspects are either all masculine signs or or all feminine signs.

The reason oppositions and square aspects are called disharmonious or unfavorable is because the signs brought together by the aspects belong to different genders.

1.14. Some Signs Command, and Others Obey

Here is a list of each sign that traditionally "commands" and the sign that "hears" or "listens" to that command:

Taurus commands, Pisces listens.

Gemini commands, Aquarius listens.

Cancer commands, Capricorn listens.

Leo commands, Sagittarius listens.

Virgo commands, Scorpio listens.

Notice that the commanding signs are spring and summer signs, when daylight is longest and nighttime the shortest. The "listening" (some astrologers say "obeying") signs are autumn and winter signs, when daylight is short and the nights are long.

Notice that Aries and Libra are not on this list. That's because when the Sun is in Aries or Libra, the daytime hours and night hours are equal in length or very near it.

1.15. Signs and Degrees that "Behold" or "Mirror"

The zodiac signs that "behold" each other are not opposite each other. Instead they "mirror" each other, because the Sun in each sign has the same amount of daylight. For both, the points on the horizon where the Sun rises and sets are also precisely the same. These signs are said to "behold" or "mirror" each other.

The five pairs of zodiac signs which "behold" each other are: Gemini-Leo, Taurus-Virgo, Aries-Libra, Pisces-Scorpio, and Aquarius-Sagittarius. These signs "mirror" each other in terms of the hours and minutes of daylight. The signs involved in these "beholding" pairings are said to have "equal power."

1.16. Disjunct Signs

Signs that are next to each other in the zodiac, and also signs that are five signs away from each other, are called "disjunct." This is why:

Signs next to each other cannot "behold" each other, cannot have a "commanding-obeying" relationship, are not of the same gender, and cannot have "equal power" in terms of daylight. They have a kind of aversion to each other.

None of the five fundamental planetary aspects—conjunction, opposition, trine, square, and sextile—can happen between signs that are adjacent or five signs away.

The planets also have other relationships with the signs. Planets can be related by house, triplicities, exaltations, and other "familiarities" I will explain later.

1.17. Planetary "Lords" or Rulers

Because the Sun's heating power is at its peak when in the signs Cancer and Leo, these two signs were assigned as their governing planets, or "lords," the planets of greatest importance: the Sun and the Moon. Together the Sun and Moon are often called "the Lights" or "the luminaries." The Sun is masculine and the Moon, feminine. These planets, closest to our Earth, have the most powerful effects on it.

Assigning the Sun and Moon to Leo and Cancer left the five other planets (Mercury, Venus, Mars, Jupiter, Saturn) to be assigned to the 10 remaining zodiac signs. Traditionally, the signs from Leo to Capricorn are "solar" and the signs from Aquarius to Cancer are "lunar."

Mercury, Venus, Mars, Jupiter and Saturn have homes in both solar and lunar signs. Thus each planet rules two zodiac signs, one solar and one lunar. And each zodiac sign, in turn, rules a planet. Signs and planets are intimately linked and these links have meaning.

The decision to link a planet with a sign was carefully made according to the planet's qualities. Because Saturn is a cold planet, it was assigned to the "solar" and "lunar" signs the Sun occupies during the coldest time of year. Therefore Saturn was assigned to Capricorn, a solar sign, and Aquarius, a lunar sign.

Capricorn and Aquarius are also diametrically opposed to the signs ruled by the Moon and Sun: Cancer and Leo. Because Saturn is the most distant planet as well as the coldest, it made sense to assign Saturn to the zodiac signs as far away as possible from—opposite—the warmest signs.

Considering the traits of each planet—whether it's hot, cold, moist or dry, or a combination—the planets are assigned to the zodiac signs according to this list:

- Aries: Mars
- Taurus: Venus
- Gemini: Mercury
- Cancer: Moon
- Leo: Sun
- Virgo: Mercury
- Libra: Venus
- Scorpio: Mars
- Sagittarius: Jupiter
- Capricorn: Saturn
- Aquarius: Saturn
- Pisces: Jupiter

Mercury, which is never more than one sign away from Sun, was given to the signs closest to the the Sun and Moon. Venus, never more than two signs away from the Sun, was assigned to the signs two signs away from the Sun and Moon. This pattern is in total and natural accord with the arrangement of the planetary spheres.

1.18. Zodiac Signs that Harmonize: Triplicities

The equilateral triangle is a harmonious shape. The 12 zodiac signs, in their circle, form a set of four triangles of three signs each. The three signs in each triangle harmonize with each other. Each triangle is called a "triplicity." So the zodiac has four "triplicities."

The first triplicity is Aries, Leo, and Sagittarius, governed by the Sun (when the horoscope is a daytime horoscope) and Jupiter (at night). This triangle is considered mostly "northern."

Aries, Leo, and Sagittarius are all masculine signs, but are not quite of the same nature because the planets they govern have different natures. Aries governs Mars, the Sun governs Leo, and Sagittarius governs Jupiter. Because the Sun creates warmth, and Jupiter is windy and fertile, these two governing planets are harmonious. Mars, though, is hot and dry, and it causes harsh winds that come from the southwest. This mixture of winds is called *Borrolibycon*.

The second triplicity is Taurus, Virgo, and Capricorn—three feminine signs. This triplicity is therefore governed by the Moon and Venus, which together are moist and warm, like the Earth.

The Moon governs this triplicity of signs by night, and Venus governs it by day. This triplicity is mostly "southern," and as I said, moist and warm. Yet Capricorn's planet is Saturn, and sometimes it will send to Earth southeastern winds called *Notapeliotes*.

The third triplicity of signs is Gemini, Libra, and Aquarius, all masculine signs. But it turns out that none of the three have any rulership over the most masculine planet, Mars. Saturn governs this triad during the day, and Mercury at night. This group is mostly "eastern," but the presence of Saturn, governed by Aquarius, can generate winds from the northeast. Jupiter is somewhat involved in this triplicity, because like Saturn it is a daytime planet. Mars is simply not involved.

The fourth triplicity is Cancer, Scorpio, and Pisces, all feminine signs. These signs are governed by the Moon, Mars, and Jupiter respectively. Even though this triad is feminine, because Scorpio's ruler is Mars this most masculine of the planets shares co-rulership with both the Moon, which governs the night, and Venus during the day. This is the "western" triplicity, but because of Venus it can also be southwestern.

1.19. Exalted and Fallen Planets

A planet is "exalted," or "in exaltation," meaning especially powerful, when it's in the zodiac sign said to be most fitting to its qualities.

The zodiac sign opposite the sign of exaltation is where that planet is least fitting, and its level of power falls low. In that sign, the planet said to be "depressed" or "fallen" or "in its fall."

To give an example, the Sun is exalted in Aries because the Sun entering Aries triggers the spring equinox, meaning that the Sun has crossed the line toward the north of the ecliptic, bringing lengthened daylight and increasingly heating Earth to its fullest extent.

When the Sun is in Libra, the Sun is heading southward. Daylight shortens and the Sun's heating power starts declining. In Libra the Sun is "depressed" or "fallen," meaning "at its weakest."

Here's a list of planets in their signs of exaltation and fall. [*The following is Ptolemy's list of planetary exaltations and falls. Because more planets have since been discovered, modern assignments are different. Ptolemy does not discuss here planets in "detriment." Today we define a planet in "detriment" as being in the zodiac sign opposite the sign it rules.*] Remember that exaltations and falls are always six signs apart, or opposites.

Planets in the signs of their "exaltation":

- Sun in Aries
- Moon in Taurus

- Mercury in Virgo
- Venus in Pisces
- Mars in Capricorn
- Jupiter in Cancer
- Saturn in Libra
- Planets in the signs of their "fall":
- Sun in Libra
- Moon in Scorpio
- Mercury in Pisces
- Venus in Virgo
- Mars in Cancer
- Jupiter in Capricorn
- Saturn in Aries

Here is the same information in table form, ordered by zodiac sign:

Sign	Exaltation	Fall
Aries	Sun	Saturn
Taurus	Moon	*None*
Gemini	*None*	*None*
Cancer	Jupiter	Mars
Leo	*None*	*None*
Virgo	Mercury	Venus
Libra	Saturn	Sun
Scorpio	*None*	Moon
Sagittarius	*None*	*None*
Capricorn	Mars	Jupiter
Aquarius	*None*	*None*
Pisces	Venus	Mercury

[*In Ptolemy's time, planets in Gemini, Leo, Sagittarius and Aquarius were neither exalted nor fallen. As the outer planets were discovered, astrologers made new and different "exalted" and "fallen" assignments.*]

Tetrabiblos

1.20. Subdividing the Signs the Egyptian Way

As we have seen, the signs have what we call planetary "lords" or "rulers" or governing planets. When a governing planet happens to be in the zodiac sign it rules, it is "at home" and most itself.

However, the Egyptians and Chaldeans both found useful a method of subdividing every zodiac sign so that different planets ruled fractions of the sign. Each subdivision is called a "term."

To explain: Each zodiac sign occupies one-twelfth of the horoscope chart, or 30 degrees out of the 360-degree circle. The ancients subdivided each one-twelfth into five consecutive sets of 6 degrees, calling these sets "terms." Each term was ruled by a different planet.

Subdivide a 30-degree span into 5 portions, and logically that should be 5 portions of 6 degrees each. But that is not how some of the ancients subdivided the houses. They said the "terms" in any one house could be as narrow as 2 degrees or as wide as 12 degrees.

Know that the terms within a sign are 1) consecutive and 2) must always total 30. Do not believe anyone who says a sign's terms total 38.5 or some other number. That cannot be right. The degrees in any one sign must always total 30. The Egyptians and Chaldeans had different methods of deciding these five terms within each sign. The Egyptians used the houses as their rationale, and the Chaldeans used the triplicities. They also disagreed on how "terms" should be interpreted. They did agree, though, that the first "term" in each sign carried more importance than the others.

Here are the planetary "terms" within the signs as they are offered to us by tradition. The "terms" together always total 30:

Aries	Jupiter 6	Venus 6	Mercury 8	Mars 5	Saturn 5
Taurus	Venus 8	Mercury 6	Jupiter 8	Saturn 5	Mars 3
Gemini	Mercury 6	Jupiter 6	Venus 5	Mars 7	Saturn 6
Cancer	Mars 7	Venus 6	Mercury 6	Jupiter 7	Saturn 4
Leo	Jupiter 6	Venus 5	Saturn 7	Mercury 6	Mars 6
Virgo	Mercury 7	Venus 10	Jupiter 4	Mars 7	Saturn 2
Libra	Saturn 6	Mercury 8	Jupiter 7	Venus 7	Mars 2
Scorpio	Mars 7	Venus 4	Mercury 8	Jupiter 5	Saturn 6
Sagittarius	Jupiter 12	Venus 5	Mercury 4	Saturn 5	Mars 4
Capricorn	Mercury 7	Jupiter 7	Venus 8	Saturn 4	Mars 4
Aquarius	Mercury 7	Venus 6	Jupiter 7	Mars 5	Saturn 5
Pisces	Venus 12	Jupiter 4	Mercury 3	Mars 9	Saturn 2

A planet, even in its home sign, is said to be be neutralized or modified by passing through another planet's "term."

1.21. Subdividing the Signs into Terms the Chaldean and Ptolemaic Ways

The Egyptian method of assigning terms has no real logic or consistency. The Chaldean method is the simpler method, based on the sequence of zodiac-sign triplicities, and makes more sense.

Here, for example, is the reasoning behind how the Chaldeans selected the planets that governed the terms of the first triplicity of signs, Aries, Leo and Sagittarius:

The Chaldeans selected Jupiter as the lord of the triplicity of Aries, Leo and Sagittarius. Jupiter therefore got first place, the most important place, among the five terms of that triplicity.

To determine the second place, the Chaldeans looked at the next triplicity, Taurus, Virgo and Capricorn. Venus was the lord of this triplicity, so they gave Venus second place among the terms.

Then they looked at the Gemini-Libra-Aquarius triplicity, and Saturn and Mercury were co-lords of this triplicity, Saturn governing the day and Mercury the night. So Saturn got the third term and Mercury the fourth.

Finally they looked at Cancer-Scorpio-Pisces triplicity, with its lords Mars and Jupiter, and gave Mars the fifth and final term.

Now the first triplicity had all its planets in place. Moving forward to the next triplicity, Taurus-Virgo-Capricorn, they assigned terms starting with Venus, lord of that triplicity, and so on down the line.

And they determined the number of degrees in each term simply by assigning the first term 8 degrees, the second term 7 degrees, the third 6 degrees, the fourth 5 degrees, and the fifth, 4 degrees. The sum of those degrees is 30, fitting each of the 12 houses perfectly.

Yet the planets do not each always get an equal number of degrees. The Chaldeans, out of all 360 degrees in a chart, assigned Saturn 78 degrees by day and 66 by night, and its co-lord Mercury 66 degrees by day and 78 by night. Venus had 75 degrees, Mars 69, and Jupiter 72.

The Egyptian system has records and examples that prove that, in practice, the Egyptian system of terms was more reliable. But those records never explain how they decided a sign's planetary terms or their order. Therefore their system is open to criticism.

The Ancient Scroll I Found

I did, however, locate and read an ancient scroll, very much damaged, and its text was very long and had too many excessively lengthy examples, but at the end of the scroll was a readable table—well protected within the scroll—that explained how the Egyptians tabulated their planetary "terms."

The Egyptians recognized the fact that the Moon and Sun aren't used in the "terms," which means the zodiac signs Cancer and Leo are deprived of their natural rulers. So the signs Cancer and Leo were assigned, for the first of their five terms, unfavorable planets—Mars to Cancer and Saturn to Leo.

Without the Moon as a participant in these terms, Venus was left as sole ruler of the triplicity of

Taurus. Other triplicities also lost their co-rulers and were assigned in their terms extra degrees that had been subtracted from the degrees allotted to the other planets. Jupiter and Saturn, slow-moving planets, lost degrees because they are slow-moving, and the degrees they lost were assigned to the planets that move more swiftly.

Here's how the scroll said to subdivide the houses for each sign [*This table of terms is now called Ptolemy's, or Ptolemaic*]:

Aries	Jupiter 6	Venus 8	Mercury 7	Mars 5	Saturn 4
Taurus	Venus 8	Mercury 7	Jupiter 7	Saturn 2	Mars 6
Gemini	Mercury 7	Jupiter 6	Venus 7	Mars 6	Saturn 4
Cancer	Mars 6	Jupiter 7	Mercury 7	Venus 7	Saturn 3
Leo	Jupiter 6	Mercury 7	Saturn 6	Venus 6	Mars 5
Virgo	Mercury 7	Venus 6	Jupiter 5	Saturn 6	Mars 6
Libra	Saturn 6	Venus 5	Mercury 5	Jupiter 8	Mars 6
Scorpio	Mars 6	Venus 7	Jupiter 8	Mercury 6	Saturn 3
Sagittarius	Jupiter 8	Venus 6	Mercury 5	Saturn 6	Mars 5
Capricorn	Venus 6	Mercury 6	Jupiter 7	Saturn 6	Mars 5
Aquarius	Saturn 6	Mercury 6	Venus 8	Jupiter 5	Mars 5
Pisces	Venus 8	Jupiter 6	Mercury 6	Mars 5	Saturn 5

Totals: Saturn 57, Jupiter 79, Mars 66, Venus 82, Mercury 76 =360.

1.22. Overthinking Places and Degrees

Some astrologers subdivided the signs even more, into twelfths, which is sections of 2-1/2 degrees each. Some assigned a term to every single degree, which makes no sense, and they assigned the planets to each degree according to the Chaldean order of terms. Their defenses of such "terms" have no foundations, so we won't discuss them.

The ancients clearly knew, because they wrote about it, how each zodiac sign is not random with random traits but naturally derived from the sign's relationship to the spring and fall equinoxes and the summer and winter solstices, and from nowhere else.

1.23. Faces, Chariots, and Other Beliefs

Such, then, are the signs and planets and their natural affinities.

There's terminology that I will define here although I do not find these concepts very useful:

A planet is said to have its "proper face" when it is the same distance from the Sun or Moon as is its natural home in the zodiac. An example: Venus has the "proper face" when it is in sextile aspect, or two signs away from, the Sun or Moon. Having the "proper face," however, also demands that

Venus is located west of the Sun and east of the Moon.

Planets are said to be in their "chariots" or "thrones" when they are in familiar or cooperative signs. Astrologers say the planets "rejoice" when in signs that aren't quite their homes but are in signs sympathetic to their sect: daytime or nighttime. The resulting effect is indirect and has less power. When planets are in an unsympathetic sect, it is as if their powers are partially paralyzed.

1.24. What the Spaces Between the Planets Mean

Let's say that in a horoscope chart there's a planet at 1 degree of Aries. If there's another planet at 6 degrees of Aries, we call the planet at 1 degree the "leading" planet and the one at 6 degrees the "following" planet.

"Leading" planets can affect those following if the "follower" is within a reasonably short distance. That distance is always measured in degrees.

There's a limit to how many degrees apart planets or points can be and still affect each other. The limit of this distance is called an "orb," short for "orb of influence."

If two planets are in conjunction, meaning they have 0 degrees between them or are up to 5 degrees apart, their powers enhance and magnify each other. (If at the same time they also happen to be in conjunction at the same or nearly the same latitude or declination, their combined power is even greater because they are "parallel" to each other as well as "in conjunction.")

Planets in a 360-degree circle are exactly aspected to each other at 0, 60, 90, 120, and 180 degrees. We allow for a few degrees, up to five, on either side of those numbers. That distance is the "orb."

Let's say Mars and Jupiter in a chart are 124 degrees apart. They are "within orb" of a trine or 120-degree aspect. "Within orb" counts when interpreting that aspect in a chart. We'd say, at 124 degrees apart, "Mars trines Jupiter." But if the aspect was exact, with Mars and Jupiter precisely 120 degrees apart, we'd give the aspect greater weight in chart interpretation. Planets approaching an aspect have more clout than they do afterward.

But please pay more attention to the planets themselves than to the spaces between them! It's the planetary vibrations which all focus and converge at our viewpoint on Earth.

From all of the above, then, we have learned that if we plan to use the zodiac signs and planets for predictions, we must:

1. Consider a planet's traits along with the character of the sign it occupies.

2. Consider a planet's relationship to the four angles: the ascendant, midheaven, descendant, or nadir, representing the sky's east, south, west, and north.

3. Consider a planet's relationship to the Sun and whether the planet is rising or setting.

4. Consider whether the planet is moving as it normally should, westward, or whether it appears to be in "retrograde" motion, moving from west to east. When in retrograde motion, a planet's power

is weakened.

5. Understand that planets have their greatest power when they are at or opposing the midheaven. They have their second-greatest power when they are exactly risen on the eastern horizon, also called the ascendant, or are within 30 degrees of rising.

6. Planets beneath the horizon, either in fact or in a horoscope chart, have less power.

7. When a planet is disjunct to the ascendant, it is powerless.

Tetrabiblos

Book Two

2.1. Introduction
2.2. How People Are Shaped by Their Environments
2.3. Nations, Their Triplicities, and Their Traits
- Europe
- Eastern Ethiopia or South Asia
- Northeast Asia
- Libya
- Where the Quarters Meet
- Quick Reference List

2.4. Making General Predictions from Eclipses
2.5. Where Will the Eclipse Have Its Greatest Impact?
2.6. Timing the Predicted Events
2.7. Who or What Will Be Affected?
2.8. The Quality and Nature of the Effect
2.9. Of the Colors of Eclipses, Comets, and Similar Phenomena
2.10. About the New Moon of the Year
2.11. How the Signs and Their Decans Affect the Weather
2.12. Investigating the Weather in Detail
2.13. About Daily and Minor Atmospheric Phenomena

2.1. Introduction

Now that we have defined the factors required for making predictions, we can discuss how to actually develop predictions, insofar as doing so is possible, while staying within the bounds of reason.

There are two categories of astrological predictions: general and specific. The general category includes the astrology of races, nations, and cities. The specific category is concerned with individuals.

It makes sense that when asked about the life of an individual we should first consider the general context he was born in or lives in.

Because this "general" category is created and swayed by greater powers, we begin with that category. We have already said this category includes large impersonal entities such as countries and cities, but let's add to those the mass calamities that happen from time to time, such as wars, famines, epidemics, earthquakes, and storms, and lesser events such as variations in the weather or crop yields.

The larger issues, such as countries of origin, of course should come first. We weigh these by looking at the signs of the zodiac, the stars in their various latitudes, the signs and houses in which the planets feel most "at home," the planets' relationships to the Sun and Moon, and their positions when rising or when turning retrograde. First we'll explain why these are significant. Then we'll discuss the national character of countries and their people as shown by their stars and signs.

2.2. How People Are Shaped by Their Environments

A nation's latitude and longitude, which are measurements made according to the ecliptic and the Sun, contribute to its particular national character, which is imparted to its people.

People in the south, specifically those who live between the equator and south of the path of the ecliptic, have black skin and thick woolly hair, short compact bodies, and have a sanguine nature. What we call "savage" about them is caused by the oppressive heat they live with. They are called, in general, "Ethiopians." Their plants and animals too show the effects of being sun-baked.

Those living in the north with the constellation Ursa Major overhead, far removed from the Sun, live in a cool but moist climate. Therefore they are white-skinned, straight-haired, tall and well-nourished. Their "savage" habits and naturally cold nature derive from living in places that are always cold. Their plants and wild animals have also been shaped or stunted by the cold. These people we call by the general name "Scythians."

Characteristics of Those Living in Temperate Zones

Those living between the hot and cold climates, in the temperate zone, definitely experience changes in temperature, but no sudden extremes. They have a medium skin color and are moderate in stature. Their temperament is balanced, and they live close together and are civilized.

Those in the southernmost part of the temperate zone are shrewder and more inventive than the others. Because they live beneath the ecliptic, the path of the planets, they know more about the heavens and things divine. They are wise, curious, and good mathematicians.

Those in the easternmost part of the temperate zone are more masculine, vigorous, straightforward, and articulate. That makes sense because living in the east, they naturally partake of the nature of the Sun. So these people are diurnal, masculine, and right-handed. Even their animals are stronger on their right sides.

Those in the west are more feminine, are soulful and speak softly, and are secretive: lunar qualities. Like the Moon they are nocturnal, feminine, and left-handed. The Moon is associated with the west because the new Moon and its crescent first show themselves in the west.

It's natural that each national group has its own specific character and customs. The places where people live encourage certain traits. Residents of countries and locales that experience climatic extremes carry the stamp of those extremes, whether it's a matter of altitude or geography.

Those living on the plains are naturally more inclined to horsemanship; coastal dwellers to seamanship; and where the soil is rich the residents incline toward settlement and civilization. In the same way, groups or nations are shaped or influenced by their particular climate and planets and signs governing that climate.

We are here speaking generally. The traits of a nation and its governing planets aren't necessarily present in every citizen. But when doing horoscopes for individuals, please recognize that their homelands' stars and planets are the backdrop for those individuals, and useful to you.

2.3. Nations, Their Triplicities, and Their Traits

[*I use the modern names of the individual countries and landmarks Ptolemy mentioned.*]

Each of the four triplicities in the zodiac is in alliance with one of the four quarters of the inhabited world. On a map, the dividing lines would run east from Gibraltar through the Taurus Mountains in southern Turkey, and from the Arabian Gulf north through the Aegean Sea to the Black Sea and the Sea of Azov.

Europe

Aries, Leo and Sagittarius is the northwest triplicity, dominated by Jupiter and the north wind, and secondarily by Mars and its southwest wind. Because this is the northwest, these planets have "occidental" or "western" traits. We call this northwestern quarter of the world "Europe."

The countries of Europe are Britain, France north of the Alps, Germany, the Celtic lands, southern Poland and southwestern Russia, Italy, Spain, and Portugal.

As one would expect, the residents of these countries have the traits of the signs that make up their triplicity, Aries, Leo, and Sagittarius, and its governing planets, Jupiter and Mars, in their occidental aspect. These people are independent, love liberty, are industrious, fond of war and weapons, clean, magnanimous, and have leadership qualities.

Because the governing planets are occidental or western, the men prefer to associate with men. Sex does not disgrace their mistresses, but the men aren't romantic or sentimental. They preserve their manliness and are helpful and benevolent. Men of good faith, they love their kin.

Traits of Europe's individual countries:

Britain, France, Germany, southern Poland and southwestern Russia are more influenced by Aries and Mars, and their inhabitants tend to be fierce, independent, headstrong, and barbaric.

Italy and northwest of Italy to the Alps, plus Apulia and Sicily, are more influenced by Leo and the Sun, so these people have mastered their work and themselves, are cooperative, and are kindly.

Tuscany, Portugal, and Spain are under the influence of Sagittarius and Jupiter, so their people show independence, simplicity, and a love of cleanliness.

Europe's largest population is concentrated in the southeastern portion of its quarter, and is therefore influenced by the signs and planets of the southeastern triplicity: Taurus, Virgo and Capricorn, and the triplicity's co-rulers Venus, Saturn, and Mercury. So the planets of both triplicities mingle their traits in these people. Residents of Macedonia, the Adriatic coast, Greece and its islands, and coastal Asia Minor are noble, clean-living, independent, democratic, creators of laws, enjoy competitive sports, music, and learning, and have leadership qualities. Through Mercury's influence they are social, friendly to visitors, eloquent, well-read, and honor the concept of justice. Because of Venus in its occidental aspect, these people can also be addicted to religious and occult mysteries and rituals.

Those living on the Greek islands, on the shores of Turkey, and in Cyprus are more influenced by Taurus and Venus, so they like luxury, and take meticulous care of their bodies. Those in or near mainland Greece and Crete, more influenced by Virgo and Mercury, are fond of reasoning and education and think their souls are more important than their bodies. Nearby, the Macedonians, Thracians, and people of the Adriatic coast, influenced by Capricorn and Saturn, are like the Greeks and Cretans except they are more acquisitive, less mannerly, and social institutions don't mean as much to them.

Eastern Ethiopia/South Asia

Taurus, Virgo and Capricorn are the southeastern triplicity. Dominating the southeast is Venus, because of the south wind, and to a lesser extent, Saturn, because of the east wind. We call this quarter of the world either eastern Ethiopia or the southern part of Greater Asia.

The countries of this quarter are India, Pakistan, Iran, and what was called Babylonia and Mesopotamia, now called Iraq. The dominant planets Venus and Saturn are oriental for this area.

This association with Venus shows in their worship of goddesses such as Isis, Astarte, or Ishtar. Saturn they worship as the god they call Mithras Helios.

These people like to divine future events. They also, uniquely, consecrate their reproductive organs. This is because their dominant planets, Venus and Saturn, are procreative. Passionate, they adore the pleasures of love and sex. Venus makes them dancers and fond of elegant and even effeminate clothes, accessories, and luxuries.

Because their dominant planets rise in the morning, the men and women carry on relations openly, but men despise the very idea of sex with other men, and most have children by their own mothers. They honor the female breast and its nearness to the heart, which is the organ governed by the Sun. The people of Iran, where the influence of Taurus and Venus is most intense, wear embroidered clothing covering the entire body except the breast.

They are clean, generous, noble, and warlike. Mesopotamians, on account of the influence of Virgo and Mercury, study mathematics and track the five planets.

Capricorn and Saturn rule the nations of India and Pakistan, and this makes the natives unattractive, grimy, and brutish.

The Arabic nations, including Syria, Chaldea, Judaea, and Arabia are in the northwest of the Eastern Asian quarter, and so have traits of the northwestern zodiac triangle of Aries, Leo, and Sagittarius and its co-rulers Jupiter, Mars, and Mercury. Compared to the others of their quarter, these people are talented businesspeople and traders, but also unscrupulous, cowards, double-crossers, servile, and fickle, because of the planets I mentioned.

The Eastern Asian people most aligned with Aries and Mars are the Syrians, Jordanians, and Judaeans: bold, scheming, and godless [*monotheistic*] people. Phoenicians, Chaldeans, and the people of the southwest Arabian coastal peninsula are aligned with Leo and the Sun. Simpler and more kindly than their neighbors, they worship the Sun and are addicted to astrology.

Those living on the Arabian peninsula are aligned with Sagittarius and Jupiter, so their country is fertile with spices, and the people are graceful, free-spirited, and good traders and businesspeople.

Northeast Asia

The Gemini, Libra and Aquarius triangle is northeastern, and its dominant planets are Saturn, because of the east wind, and to a lesser extent Jupiter, because of the north wind. This quarter covers the northern part of Greater Asia. It includes Armenia, Central Asia, the Caucasus, the area around the Caspian Sea, western China, Asiatic Russia, and all the other nations in the northeastern part of the world. They are governed by the planets Saturn and Jupiter, in their oriental or eastern aspect. Wealthy, clean, religious, affectionate, noble enough to die for their friends or a holy cause, they hate evil. Regarding sex, they are pure and dignified. Jupiter's and Saturn's governance makes them well-dressed, and warm and generous hosts.

Armenians and those living south of the Caspian Sea are allied with Gemini and Mercury, so they are more highly strung and can be mischievous. Libra and Venus influence those living north of the Caspian Sea, in Central Asia, and in China, so those people like luxuries and the arts. The people ruled by Aquarius and Saturn, farther northeast, are brusque, humorless, and barbaric.

Those in this quarter who live nearest the center of the inhabited world, the Syrians and inhabitants of Asia Minor, inhabit the southwest corner of their quarter, and so are influenced by the triplicity of Cancer, Scorpio, and Pisces, with the planets Mars, Venus, and Mercury governing them. They worship Venus under many names as the mother of their gods, and Mars or Adonis as her consort. The women obey their husbands and are good housekeepers, but the men are models of depravity: mercenary, warring, looting, and enslaving even their own people. On the northern coast of Turkey the sign Cancer rules, and the Moon, so the men are the obedient caretakers and the women militant and distinctly unfeminine Amazons who cut off their right breasts to better handle their weaponry. They'll display these scars to enemies to warn them that those they are about to fight are not typical females.

Scorpio and Mars influence the area west of Armenia, and parts of Syria. Bold and treacherous swindlers, they are also hard workers. Pisces and Jupiter are allied with the people of southern Turkey, and those are wealthier and more social, and trustworthy about fulfilling their business contracts.

Libya

Cancer, Scorpio, and Pisces form the southwestern triplicity, dominated by Mars because of the dry west wind, and Venus to a lesser extent because of the south wind. The quarter associated with this triplicity is called Libya or western Ethiopia. It includes the North African nations west of the Nile.

Because Mars and Venus are their rulers, these nations are in general ruled by a brother and sister who are married, and this pattern continues through the generations. The man rules the men and the woman rules the women. The men here often kidnap their brides, and their king will demand for himself the virginity of newly married women. Some of the women are the equivalent of public property. Although Venus influences the men to dress up and wear jewelry, they are still masculine, and can be fakers, liars, and reckless.

The people in the sector which includes Carthage are influenced by Cancer and the Moon and are affluent, sociable, and business-minded. Those of the area including Algeria and Mauritania, ruled by Scorpio and Mars, are carnivores, do not value life, and kill each other mercilessly. Those living in south and southwestern Libya are Jupiterian and Piscean, making them willing workers, freedom-loving, independent, and clean, and worshippers of Jupiter whom they call Ammon.

In the northeastern part of this quarter, nearest the center of the inhabited world, places such as Egypt, the Sinai peninsula, Arabia, and Somaliland are ruled by the northeastern triplicity of Gemini, Libra, and Aquarius. The influence here of Saturn, Jupiter and Mercury, all here occidental, makes them religious, superstitious, performers of elaborate rituals and burials and rites of mourning, and believers in numerous gods. As subjects they are docile, timid, and long-suffering, and their leaders courageous and generous. But they are all lustful and take multiple wives and multiple husbands, and will marry their siblings. Both the men and women are extra fertile, as is their land. Some of the men are deeply effeminate, and some of these are contemptuous of all reproductive organs when occidental Venus aspects the unfavorable planets.

Inhabitants of the areas along the Red Sea and Lower Egypt are influenced by Gemini and Mercury, and therefore are thoughtful and intelligent seekers of wisdom. They perform secret rituals and magic, and are talented mathematicians. The people on the Red Sea's west coast, under the influence of Libra and Venus, are passionate, lively, and live comfortably. The nomads of Arabia and the residents of the southeastern African coast eat meat and fish and live hard and barbarous lives.

Where the Quarters Meet

The great cities of each quarter of the inhabited world are near the place where the quarters meet, and this central region is governed by Mercury.

Quick Reference List

Here for quick reference is a list of zodiac signs and the nations associated with them:

Aries: Britain, France, Germany, Syria, Palestine, Jordan, and Israel.

Taurus: northeastern Iran, the Greek islands, Cyprus, and coastal Turkey/Asia Minor.

Gemini: Armenia, Iran, coastal Libya, lower Egypt, southeast of the Caspian Sea, and the Caucasus.

Cancer: Algeria, Carthage, east central Turkey, the eastern coast of the Black Sea.

Leo: Italy, the area of Italy southeast of the Alps, Sicily and the "heel" of Italy's "boot," southwestern Turkey, and Chaldea.

Virgo: Iraq [*including the former Babylonia and Mesopotamia*], mainland Greece, and Crete.

Libra: Central Asia, the Caspian Sea area, China, and Somaliland.

Scorpio: Algeria, Mauritania, Syria, and east central Asia Minor.

Sagittarius: Italy along the Tyrrhenian Sea, France northwest of the Alps, Spain, and the rich lands of Arabia.

Capricorn: India, Pakistan, Macedonia, and the Balkan coast along the Adriatic.

Aquarius: Russia, Arabia, the southeastern African coast, and Middle Ethiopia.

Pisces: southwestern Libya, Algeria, the Sahara, southern Turkey, and the western half of Asia Minor.

Each of the fixed stars—those just north or south of the ecliptic—has a sympathetic relationship with each country as well.

If a major city was founded at a known date and time, a "natal" horoscope can be cast for it, and the Sun and Moon placements will count the most in that horoscope. When the date and time are not known, use as the city's "natal" horoscope the natal horoscope of the city's founder, or the king or leader at that time, and look at that horoscope's midheaven. The sign at the midheaven of the chart is the city's ruling zodiac sign.

2.4. Making General Predictions from Eclipses

Now it's time to discuss briefly how to make predictions, and first, before doing anything else, we address what we have called the general predictions, concerning whole regions, countries or cities.

By far the most significant factors in predictions for countries and cities are the Sun and Moon and especially their eclipses and the positions of the planets at the time of an eclipse. In these lie the cause or causes of the events to come.

Second in significance are the stations of Saturn, Jupiter, and Mars. It is significant when and where these planets seem to halt in the sky while preparing to change direction.

To predict a future event, what an astrologer will want to ascertain, in order, is 1) the region or locale that will be affected by the future event; 2) the hour and duration of that predicted event; 3) what things or people will be most affected; and 4) the event's main or signature quality. That last one can be determined by the specific planetary aspects occurring at the time of the eclipse. Let's take the four steps one at a time.

2.5. Where Will the Eclipse Have Its Greatest Impact?

Before deciding what kind of event we will predict, we must first determine where, geographically, the eclipse will have its greatest impact. Individual eclipses are not visible everywhere on Earth, so only those regions, countries, or cities that can actually witness the eclipse will be affected by it.

Determine what zodiac sign the eclipse is in, and which sign of the zodiac will be rising in the east during the eclipse, and where the Sun and Moon will be.

The sign the eclipse is in is, of course, part of a triplicity. The countries that match that triplicity are the sites potentially affected. All matching countries might be affected by the eclipse in some way, but for your prediction you can greatly narrow the field by finding out which countries or cities will actually witness the eclipse.

As an alternative, use the "natal" horoscope for the city or country, if you have it, and look at its Sun and Moon positions as they relate to the eclipse point. Or use the natal horoscope of the city's founder or first leader, if you have it, and note the zodiac sign on that chart's midheaven. See how that sign relates to the sign the eclipse occurs in.

All cities with astrological links to the zodiac sign the eclipse occurs in will be affected, but most especially those that will witness the eclipse. List those locales. Now you have pinned down the locales that will experience the events the eclipse portends.

2.6. Timing the Predicted Events

Next, determine the timing and length of the event you want to foresee. Consider that:

a total eclipse in one locale will be seen as a partial eclipse at a locale at another latitude.

the eclipse's duration will vary in each locale.

Find out for each important locale the times the eclipse starts and ends. Set up a horoscope for each place using the eclipse's date, time, and place as your foundation, as you would for a person's natal horoscope.

The eclipse's duration will allow you to predict how long the future event will last. Here's how you find that. Calculations for lunar and solar eclipses will differ.

A lunar eclipse can last up to two hours. A solar eclipse lasts a maximum of eight minutes. To make a prediction, we must know how many degrees the Earth turns during a lunar or solar eclipse. The Earth turns approximately 15 degrees per hour, as measured from its equator.

As an example, let's say a lunar eclipse lasts a full two hours. In two hours the Earth turns approximately 30 degrees. For a lunar eclipse, we then match the number of degrees with the same number of months. The answer for how long this future event will last, then, is "30 months."

Solar eclipses last mere minutes, so we must do fractions. As an example, let's say the solar eclipse at your selected locale lasts four minutes. In one minute the Earth turns one-quarter of one degree. So in four minutes the Earth will turn one degree.

For solar eclipse predictions, we match the number of degrees with a number of years. With a four-minute solar eclipse, during which the Earth turns one degree, we calculate that the event we hope to predict will last for one year.

To figure out when the event we hope to predict will begin, we look at the chart of our selected locale and where the eclipse takes place relative to its horizon. If the eclipse takes place anywhere from the eastern horizon to the first third of the sky the answer is: The event will happen within four months from the time of the eclipse. If the eclipse in that sector happens to take place close to the eastern horizon, the most intense portion of the event will take place within the first third of those four months, or within 40 days following the eclipse.

If the eclipse took place in the middle third of the sky, on either side of the midheaven, the event will take place five to eight months after the eclipse, and its effect will be most intense about six months after the eclipse.

If it took place in the western third of the sky, the event will happen nine months to a year after the eclipse. That event will be at its peak intensity if the eclipse occurs in the final third of those four months.

The planetary aspects during each four-month sector, especially aspects involving the Sun and Moon, will tell us more precisely when an event will begin and when its effects will crest or diminish. Aspects to planets that are rising or stationary will create increasing intensity, and planets that are setting, or evening planets, will allow matters to abate.

2.7. Who or What Will Be Affected?

We can predict who or what in general will be affected by the eclipse by looking 1) at the planets in the zodiac sign where the eclipse occurs, and 2) at the zodiac sign in which we find the angle that precedes the eclipse. Remember that the four angles in a horoscope chart are the ascendant, midheaven, descendant, and nadir.

Now you must find the planetary lord of the eclipse. No, it is not as simple as saying, "The planetary lord of the eclipse has to be the lord of the sign the eclipse is in." That might not be true at all. Follow this train of thought:

Consider the nature and qualities of the zodiac sign that contains the eclipse, and then the planets and fixed stars that happen to be in that sign.

Then look at the positions of the planets and fixed stars that govern or are lords of that zodiac sign, and their relationships to the eclipse point. Are the aspects between the planets favorable, or are they unfavorable?

Look then at the zodiac sign containing the angle preceding the eclipse, and at the planets and fixed stars in that sign. Find out where that sign's governing planets and fixed stars happen to be at the time of the eclipse. Are the aspects between the planets favorable or unfavorable?

You still have several more factors to weigh before deciding which planets actually do govern the eclipse. Look at the signs and planets linked to the eclipse point, perhaps by triplicity. Planetary powers are enhanced if they are linked to the eclipse point.

If one planet clearly plays multiple roles, that planet dominates or is lord the eclipse. The lord of the nearest angle plays a secondary or co-rulership role.

If multiple planets are contending for those roles, choose either the planet closest to the nearest angle, or the planet having the most governance over the locale.

If a prominent fixed star rises at the time of the eclipse, or at that time culminates at the angle following that eclipse, that star's particular powers, and the sign that it is in, must be factored into the prediction. If that star is rising, its powers are enhanced.

Now, with all these factors weighed and decided, you are ready to predict who or what will be actually affected by the eclipse.

- If the planets and fixed stars most involved are in constellations that look like human beings, such as Virgo the Virgin or Aquarius the Water Bearer, the event will chiefly affect the human race.

- If the planets and fixed stars most involved are in constellations of four-footed animals, such as Aries the Ram or Taurus the Bull, the event will most affect four-footed animals.

- If the signs Aquarius or Pisces are heavily involved, the event will affect river- and ocean-dwelling creatures, especially those we eat.

- If the planets or the most prominent fixed stars are in zodiac signs resembling sheep, horses or oxen, domesticated animals are the most affected.

- If the planets or the most prominent fixed stars are in the zodiac signs representing wild and dangerous animals, such as Leo the Lion, those are the animals most affected.

- If the planets or most prominent fixed stars are in constellations that resemble creeping things, such as Scorpio or Cancer, those kinds of animals will be most affected.

- The above also applies to constellations outside of the zodiac. For example, when the stars involved are in or near constellations shaped like winged creatures, such as the constellations Cygnus the Swan and Aquila the Eagle, winged creatures will be most affected, especially those we eat.

- If the fixed stars involved are in the far-northern constellations outside of the zodiac, expect earthquakes. If they are in far-southern constellations outside of the zodiac, expect heavy rain.

Check whether the planets most involved in the eclipse are in the equinoctial signs (Aries and Libra) or the solstitial signs (Cancer and Capricorn). If in Aries, the sign of the spring equinox, plants such as budding fig trees and young grapevines will be affected by the event. In Libra, the event will affect the grains and herbs usually planted or harvested in early autumn. If in Cancer, sign of the summer solstice, ripening vegetables and fruits will be affected, and the event will probably interfere with the annual flooding of the Nile. If in Capricorn, root vegetables, fish, and other creatures most common in that season will be affected.

Dominant stars and planets that happen to be in Aries and Libra tend to have have significant effects on religious rites and worship of the gods. If they are in Cancer or Capricorn, expect changes in weather and politics. If in Taurus, Leo, Scorpio, and Aquarius, the solid signs, expect changes in institutions and the foundations of buildings; and if in the double-bodied or bicorporeal signs of Gemini, Virgo, Sagittarius, and Pisces, the future event will affect royals and their subjects.

Ruling planets and stars near the eastern horizon mean that the event will mostly affect young people, seeds and fruits, and emerging institutions. Near the midheaven, they will affect religion, established royalty and dynasties, and the middle-aged. Near the descendant, they will influence changing customs, the elderly, and the dead.

The percentage of people, animals, things, or institutions affected depends on whether the eclipse was, at that locale, a full or partial eclipse. If it was partial, we ask what percentage of the Sun or Moon was eclipsed. The locales that experience total eclipses are affected the most.

A solar eclipse's effect is much stronger, and the effect will last longer, if the ruling signs and planets are to the east of the eclipse point, and much weaker if they are to the west. A lunar eclipse is much stronger if the signs and planets most involved are to its west, and much weaker if they are to its east.

2.8. The Quality and Nature of the Effect

The fourth and final issue to address is whether the event's effect will be favorable or unfavorable.

To figure this, we must consider all the previous factors such as 1) the eclipse point, 2) the sign it is in, 3) the planets ruling the locale, 4) the eclipse's ruling signs and planets, and 5) the fixed stars involved. The Sun and Moon dominate an eclipse's horoscope and either strengthen or weaken the ruling planets.

Each of the five other planets has particular qualities. When predicting an eclipse's effect we rely on the qualities of the signs, planets, and fixed stars involved. Note that my examples here are of the planets as if they were the sole rulers of an eclipse. Adjust your reading to its particular blend of rulers.

If Saturn clearly is lord of the eclipse and its fixed stars, disasters and diseases related to cold will follow. A dominant Saturn might bring afflictions related to cold, such as tuberculosis, wasting, arthritis, colds, exile, poverty, and deaths, but mostly of the elderly. Animals too will get sick and spread diseases. The air will be cold and gloomy, with snowstorms and hailstorms that later generate poisonous insects and reptiles. Expect tempests at sea that wreck ships and fishing. Flooding, insects and blights might affect crops and bring the threat of famine.

If Jupiter is clearly the sole lord of the eclipse, things in general are on the increase and humanity will benefit. Peace, comfort, health, prosperity, fulfillment of all human needs, and benevolent kings and rulers are among Jupiter's gifts. Spiritual and physical health are heightened. Domestic and service animals will thrive while hostile wild animals decline and die. The weather will be gentle, not extreme, with just enough moisture, and excellent for abundant crops.

If Mars is ultimately the governor of the eclipse, drought will follow and humanity engage in wars, destruction, and enslavement. Kings will hate their subjects and vice versa. Mars brings sudden death and fevers and hemorrhages that cause painful deaths, especially among those in their prime. Violent crime of all types will flourish. Hot winds which dry up and deplete rivers and springs will be followed by terrific storms and hurricanes. Crops and livestock cannot survive these extremes. Harvests are lost to fire or are spoiled by excessive heat, and drinking water is tainted. Ships at sea meet with storms.

If Venus dominates the eclipse, it brings benefits like Jupiter's, only sweeter. A dominant Venus brings fame and honors, and supports good relationships, fruitful marriages, and generally civilized and congenial behavior. People will show appropriate reverence to religious institutions. Rulers are benevolent, make good alliances, and prosper. The air is pure and healthy, freshened by cool, moist breezes that bring enough rainfall for crops and livestock to thrive. Ships make safe and profitable journeys. All these good things in abundance will encourage people to be joyful.

If Mercury rules the eclipse, the eclipse has a stimulating influence. When Mercury is lord, you can predict that men will be sharp thinkers, practical, and ingenious. But Mercury often takes on the nature of planets in aspect with it, and if those planets are unfavorable, the people suffer assault, piracy, theft, business losses, drought, tuberculosis and coughing. Mercury as lord will trigger events pertaining to religion and theology, laws and customs, and taxes in accordance with the planets in aspect with it. Because it is close to the Sun, Mercury's nature is dry and windy, and brings unpredictable and sometimes disastrous weather, and also earthquakes. Rivers and other waters diminish as this dry planet sets, and rise when Mercury rises.

Those are the effects the five planets generate on their own. However, their aspects with other planets and signs create different effects. There are so many possible configurations that confidently matching each one with an exact prediction and listing them all here for you would be a hopeless task, best left to those astrologers who qualify as mathematicians.

An eclipse's effect on a country or city is related to the planets that govern the eclipse. If they are:

- favorable planets
- in harmony with the planets governing the locale, and
- aren't affected by planets to the west of them (called "superior" planets) that can skew their effects
- they will be beneficial to the locale.

If the planets and locale don't harmonize much, expect the eclipse to be less helpful. If they don't harmonize at all, expect disasters. In that case, the most unfortunate people will be the individuals who in their natal horoscopes have the Sun or Moon at the sign or degree of the eclipse, or in opposition to that degree.

2.9. Of the Colors of Eclipses, Comets, and Similar Phenomena

For predicting general conditions, we must also observe that eclipses sometimes generate beams of light or halos of certain colors. Phenomena which are black or darkly mottled have Saturn's qualities. The color white has Jupiter's qualities. Red is Mars, yellow is Venus, and multi-colored, Mercury.

If the particular color covers most of the Sun or Moon or the area around it, the eclipse's effects will cover most of the country or countries involved in the prediction. If the coloration is partial, it will affect the part of the country in which the phenomenon's display is most intense.

Comets bring with them the disturbing effects of Mars and Mercury: wars, hot weather, and sudden changes. A comet causes troubles in the nations or regions governed by the zodiac signs in which you see the comet's head and its tail. The comet also points itself toward the region to be most affected.

When comets appear to the east of the Sun, they announce events soon to come, and to the west of the Sun they announce events that will take more time to unfold. The way the comet's head is shaped indicates the type of event it will be and the earthly creatures who will be affected. The duration of the comet foretells the duration of the event.

2.10. About the First New Moon of the Year

Now that we have explained how to predict events in countries and cities, we will go into more detail and address annual or seasonal events.

First, let's discuss the first new Moon of the year. When that occurs depends on where you say your year begins. Take your choice of the solstices or equinoxes, as did the ancients, and that still leaves all the other points. Technically you could choose any point as the starting point of your year. The Egyptian year, for example, began at the summer solstice, as the Dog Star rose, signaling the annual flooding of the Nile. You could choose the autumn equinox because at that time crops are harvested and the seeds for next year's crop are sown.

The solstices and equinoxes, because they are derived from the Sun, are traditionally the chosen starting points because each signals the start of a new season. The summer and winter solstices take place in Cancer and Capricorn, and the spring and autumn equinoxes in Aries and Libra. Of the four of these, the spring equinox most has the natural qualities of a beginning.

From the qualities of each of these signs we can predict the winds and temperatures the season will bring. You can predict variations on the weather and temperature by looking at the planetary aspects to the equinox and solstice points.

Yet it seems to me even more rewarding to assess the weather on a monthly basis by studying the charts of new Moons and full Moons occurring monthly in each of the zodiac signs and the signs opposite—most especially the full Moons just preceding any of the four angles in a horoscope chart.

2.11. How the Signs and Their Decans Affect the Weather

In Book One, chapters 4 and 18, we discussed the powers of the planets, zodiac signs, and fixed stars to influence winds and weather conditions. Now let's talk in more detail about the nature of the signs as a whole and the weather they bring, and the details we can learn about the weather when the zodiac signs are each subdivided into into thirds: portions of 10 degrees each.

[*Ptolemy doesn't call these 10-degree portions "decans," but the concept is the same. Some astrologers call the decans "faces," but Ptolemy's definition of "proper faces" in Book One, chapter 23, has nothing to do with "decans."*]

Aries: This equinoctial sign as a whole brings thunder or hail. Its first decan, or the first one-third of it, as it rises brings rain and winds. The middle decan brings fair weather, and its final decan brings heat and pestilence. The part of Aries north of the ecliptic brings destructive heat, and to the south of the ecliptic, frost and cold.

Taurus: The sign as a whole is temperate, but on the warm side. Its first decan, or the first one-third of it containing the Pleiades, as it rises brings earthquakes, wind, and fog. The middle decan brings wet, cold weather, and its final decan containing the star cluster called the Hyades brings thunder and lightning. The part of Taurus north of the ecliptic brings destructive heat, and to the south of the ecliptic, unstable and unpredictable weather.

Gemini: The sign as a whole brings temperatures neither too hot nor too cold. Its first decan, or the first one-third of it as it rises, brings excessive rain. The middle decan brings fair weather, and its final decan brings unexpected or mixed weather. The part of Gemini north of the ecliptic brings winds and earthquakes, and to the south of the ecliptic, dryness and drought.

Cancer: The sign as a whole brings fine, fair summer weather, but its first decan, or the first one-third of it as it rises, containing the star cluster called "The Beehive," is humid and triggers earthquakes. The middle and the third decan both bring winds. The parts of Cancer north and south of the ecliptic brings destructive heat and drought.

Leo: The sign as a whole brings oppressive heat. Its first decan, or the first one-third of it as it rises, brings heat and pestilence. The middle decan brings fair weather, and its final decan is windy. Leo north of the ecliptic brings stifling and unstable weather, and to the south of the ecliptic, Leo generates moisture.

Virgo: This zodiac sign as a whole is damp or wet and prone to thunderstorms. Its first decan, or the leading one-third of it as it rises, is warm and harsh. The middle decan is temperate, and its final decan, wet. The part of Virgo north of the ecliptic brings winds, and to the south of the ecliptic, fair and seasonable weather.

Libra: Under this sign, any kind of weather might happen. Its first and second decans, or the first two-thirds as they rise, encourage fair weather. The final decan is wet. The part of Libra north of the ecliptic is windy, and to the south of the ecliptic, wet and unhealthy.

Scorpio: The sign as a whole brings thunder or fire. Its first decan, or the first one-third of it as it rises, can bring snow. The middle decan brings fair weather, and its final decan causes earthquakes. The part of Scorpio north of the ecliptic is hot and to the south of it, moist.

Sagittarius: This zodiac sign as a whole is windy. Its first decan, or the first one-third of it as it rises, brings precipitation. The middle decan is temperate, and its final decan fiery. The part of Sagittarius north of the ecliptic is windy, and to the south of the ecliptic the weather will be wet and threatening.

Capricorn: This sign as a whole has a moist character. Its first decan, or the first one-third of it as it rises, brings damaging heat. The middle decan and final decan both bring stormy weather. Capricorn's stars both north and south of the ecliptic are wet and damaging.

Aquarius: This sign as a whole is cold and watery. Its first decan, or the first one-third of it as it rises, is damp. The middle decan brings fair weather appropriate to the season, and its final decan brings winds. The part of Aquarius north of the ecliptic brings heat, and to the south of the ecliptic, cloudy skies.

Pisces: The sign as a whole is cold and windy, but its first one-third of it as it rises brings good weather. The middle decan is moist, and its final decan brings heat. The part of Pisces north of the ecliptic brings winds, and the south of the ecliptic, watery weather.

2.12. Investigating the Weather in Detail

Now I will describe what all these facts together signify for predicting the weather for each quarter of the year, using the new or full Moons occurring prior to the Sun's contact with the solstice or equinox points.

One way to do this is to find the degrees of the new and full Moons that most closely precede the solstitial and equinoctial signs, at the latitude of the locale that interests us. We use these degrees as the angles of our chart. Just as we did with eclipses, we note and analyze the signs, planets, fixed stars and their aspects to one another at that locale at that time. By compiling this information we can predict the general properties of the coming season's weather. The planetary rulers of these degrees, and stars ruling this new or full Moon, will reveal the properties and natures of any extremes or shadings in the weather of the coming season.

You can make monthly weather predictions for the season using charts for the new Moon or the full Moon for that lunar month, but you must choose between the new Moon or full Moon and stick with it for that whole season.

The points marking the lunar month's new Moon and full Moon are always points of interest. Each one is worth its own full horoscope chart, taking all stars, signs, planets, and their aspects to each other, into consideration. The previous chapter described the weather by the zodiac signs and their decans, so use that information too. Compare your results with the current weather. You can then predict the general weather conditions for the coming month.

To predict the weather in more detail, consider the Moon's quarter phases. About three days before and sometimes up to three days after a Sun-Moon conjunction, a certain variation in the atmosphere might begin, and the quarter moons intensify or diminish it. Notice any trine or sextiles that the Moon, in its quarter phase, is making to the other planets. The nature of these planets and their signs indicate the particular quality of the change in weather.

The qualities you discern in the weather will manifest more fully on days when the brighter and more powerful fixed stars are close to the Sun, whether like morning stars they are east of the Sun or rising, or like evening stars, to west of the Sun and setting. The weather can take on qualities associated with each of these fixed stars, especially when the Sun or Moon is passing over one of the angles. Fixed stars are able to intensify or diminish weather conditions hour by hour, just as the tides respond to Moon phases. When the Sun and Moon are on the angles, the Moon's declinations in particular can change the winds toward the direction the Moon is traveling.

Remember, the most important and primary causes are the general ones, and the specific ones are secondary. The secondary conditions can be solidly confirmed when the planets and stars support both the general conditions and the specific ones.

2.13. About Daily and Minor Atmospheric Phenomena

It's useful, when making predictions, to observe the zodiac signs that the Sun, Moon, and other planets are in.

At sunrise we can determine the day's weather, and at sunset, the night's weather. Look at the Sun's aspects to the Moon to predict weather for a span of time longer than a day.

The weather will be fair during the day and the night when the Sun rises and sets without being surrounded or obscured by clouds or mists. If the Sun is obscured only in the evening, the night's weather will not be as fair as the daytime's. The Sun's aspect to the Moon will determine how likely it is that the current weather will continue. The current weather conditions are likely to persist until the Sun or Moon makes aspects to the other planets.

When the rising Sun has reddish or yellowish clouds around it or sends out long rays, expect violent winds to arise from the angles associated with the Sun's and Moon's positions in the zodiac signs.

A pale or sickly-looking Sun surrounded by clouds or halos indicates winds and storms.

A darkly mottled Sun, or dark rays from the Sun, indicate rough weather.

Observe the Moon three days before or after the new Moon, and also in its full and quarter phases. Weather will be fine if the Moon on those nights shines brightly and clearly. A reddish Moon, or a pale one, or one clearly showing the parts of the Moon that should be in darkness, means winds will be coming from the direction of the Moon's declination. A bloated-looking Moon, one with clouds muffling it on both sides, or a dark Moon, indicate rainstorms.

A single crisp and clear halo around the Moon means fair weather. More than one halo means storms are coming. Reddish or broken halos foretell wild winds, thrashing seas, and possibly hurricanes. If the halo is broken or black, expect snow mixed with rain. The more halos, the more furious the storms will be.

Planets and fixed stars sometimes have halos. Colored halos have effects appropriate to their colors, and also have effects depending on the natures of the Sun and Moon, if those are nearby.

The colors of the planets and fixed stars also have meaning. Stars that seem larger and brighter than usual foretell that winds will be blowing from that direction.

Observe too the nebulous objects such as The Beehive cluster in the zodiac sign Cancer. If even on a clear night they appear cloudy, rain is coming. If the stars are distinctly separate and they twinkle, expect clear weather.

Comets cause drought, and they cause winds. The larger the comet, the harsher the winds will be.

The trails of shooting stars or meteors, when those trails are short, indicate winds will arrive from the same direction the meteor is traveling in. A long-tailed meteor brings disastrously stormy weather. Meteors flying in all different directions stir the winds and bring very heavy weather.

Fluffy clouds sometimes generate terrific storms. Rainbows during storms calm the weather. A rainbow visible during good weather means storms are brewing.

Everything visible in the sky portends what is to come, and reveals the event's cause and effects. In the following pages, we will discuss how to make predictions for and about people, using their birth charts.

Tetrabiblos

Book Three

3.1. What We Are Born With

3.2. Pinpointing the Ascendant

3.3. Questions a Natal Horoscope Can Answer

3.4. About the Parents and Planetary "Attendants"

3.5. About Brothers and Sisters

3.6. Predicting a Baby's Gender

3.7. Predicting Twins or Multiple Births

3.8. Birth Defects

3.9. Babies That Die, are Given Up, or Abandoned

3.10. Figuring the Potential Lifespan

3.11. An Example of Lifespan Calculation

3.12. Looks and Temperament

3.13. About Sicknesses and Injuries

3.14. The Quality of the Character

3.15. Of Diseases of the Soul

3.1. What We Are Born With

Book Two described the causes of global events, such as weather. Individual horoscopes, those we cast for people, must be judged along with the universal backdrop provided by the planets, stars, and environmental conditions.

To make predictions, astrologers scientifically observe the heavens in flux and how that continual activity and change compares with or parallels events on Earth. The planets, including the Sun and Moon, and the stars are all continually in motion and are the source of every event, whether general or specific.

When making predictions for individuals from birth charts, consider the backdrop as important as the individual. If anything, in your predictions the universal forces should carry more weight because they act independently of humanity and are stronger than we are. Interpreting the general or universal horoscope requires more than simply noting what sign rises over the horizon during the time in question. Unlike people, the universe has no single birthplace or birth time, so there is no starting point that determines all the other points. For the universal horoscope there are many possible starting points, such as a full solar eclipse's date, place and time, or a significant point in a planet's path of travel.

When making predictions for a person, we have one primary starting point. Within the zodiac sign rising at the date, time and place of birth, there is one point that was exactly on the eastern horizon. This is the ascendant point. This primary starting point determines all the other points in a person's chart, which determine a person's physical and spiritual traits, so the ascendant is the most important point. For other kinds of horoscopes we might choose other starting points, such as in horary astrology where we choose as our chart's starting point the moment the individual asks the question.

Ideally, astrologers would like to begin drawing up a person's chart using the time and locale of the person's conception, because that is when a human being first acquires substance, and that substance naturally attracts more of the same substance, and so on. Unfortunately, most of us don't know where and when we were conceived. So astrology has chosen the moment of birth instead. Conception could be called "the source," and birth could be called "the beginning." Both starting points are about equally good for making horoscopes, with a conception chart having this advantage: From a conception chart we could predict incidents that happen before birth. A lot can happen between conception and birth as seed is transformed into a growing fetus.

Regardless of which aspects rule the skies, know these two things: that a child is always born when it should be, and that the birth or natal horoscope will in some way echo the conception horoscope.

Let me emphasize, as I did in Book One, that natal stars and planets do not determine or generate life events. Rather, they reveal the individual's potential, and the potential for future life events. Only in that way can we say the natal horoscope is a cause of future life events.

I will not in this book describe the ancient method of prediction which took into account almost all the stars and astral phenomena. Its complexity could be infinite. The ancients observed nature directly, working from square one with no treasury of traditions to help build useful theories. We have those theories now, and will use them in our more practical method of prediction, which includes a reasonable amount of thoughtful conjecture, and is always in harmony with the laws of nature.

I will discuss where to look in the heavens for portents of future events and the factors involved in summing them all up into a prediction, but in this book will not make actual predictions. I leave that to those who are sufficiently skilled and motivated.

We will use birth data, because they give us all we need. If you have access to a conception chart, use it to supplement birth data.

3.2. Pinpointing the Ascendant

The first thing astrologers will have to know is the hour and minute of a birth. Yet because our sundials and water clocks cannot reliably measure fractions of an hour, all we usually have to start with is the hour of birth. With only the birth hour, how can we calculate the exact degree of the zodiac rising at the moment of birth—the ascendant point so basic to the natal horoscope chart—when earth's rotation changes the ascendant by one degree every four minutes?

To determine that degree it would have been best if we had owned and used an astrolabe at the birth time and place, but chances are we did not, so our best approximation will have to do. If we know the birth hour, by using the Doctrine of Ascensions we can find the zodiac sign rising at the minute of birth, also called the rising sign or ascendant.

[*Ptolemy doesn't explain here the Doctrine of Ascensions. The Table of Latitude and Table of Ascension required to complete the calculation are in his astronomy text* The Almagest. *In the computer era, enter birth and locale information into an online "rising sign calculator," or use astrological software. Having the time of birth, to the minute, yields the correct rising sign and the exact degree of it that was rising. Ptolemy briefly describes in the paragraphs below his method of calculating that degree when a person's birth time is not known.*]

After finding the zodiac sign that was rising, determine its degree on the horizon using this process. First, look at the individual's birth date. Find the new Moon or full Moon preceding the birth—whichever of those occurred closest to the birth. The sign and degree of that Moon will also show you the degree of the Sun: At a full Moon, the Sun is directly opposite the Moon. At a new Moon, the Sun and Moon are at the same degree.

In case the full Moon occurred beneath the horizon, use the degree of the Sun. When in doubt, always choose the degree of the luminary that was above the horizon at the time.

Determine the planet or planets that dominated this degree at the time of the birth. There are five ways to judge this. A planet with a clear and definite majority of those contacts is unquestionably the chart's dominant planet. See:

- whether a planet was in trine aspect to that degree

- whether a planet is exalted within its zodiac sign
- which house that planet occupies
- what "term" the planet belongs to in the house it occupies
- and its phase or aspect in relation to the planet that dominates the birth locale.

That dominant planet's degree is the one you should choose. Find that same degree in the sign you determined was rising. That degree of that sign is the person's ascendant—the starting point for setting up the horoscope.

If two or more planets each have an equal number of contacts or dignities with that particular degree, they are co-rulers of the chart, but in this case when we are seeking a single ascendant point we must narrow those down to one planet. Choose the planet closest to the ascendant.

It sometimes happens that the ruling planet is very distant from the ascendant. If it is farther away from the midheaven than it is from the ascendant, use the ruling planet's sign and degree as the midheaven or zenith of the chart. From there you can establish a new ascendant point for setting up the horoscope.

3.3. Questions a Natal Horoscope Can Answer

There are four categories of predictions for individuals. They are:

1. Events before the birth: for example, events that involved the parents.

2. Events related to the birth, such as the births of siblings.

3. Events happening at the time of birth. Predicting or identifying those isn't as simple or straightforward for us as it was for the ancients, as I will explain.

4. Events after birth. Predicting those isn't simple or straightforward either, because the methods of prediction are better developed and more complex than they used to be.

During a pregnancy, people will eagerly ask an astrologer about the baby's gender, whether it could be twins, if the baby will be normal and healthy, and whether the baby will live to be raised by its parents or someone else.

After a birth, people ask how long the individual will live (predictable only after the baby's first year and if the baby was born healthy) and what he or she will grow up to look like. They ask about possible injuries and illnesses; whether he or she will be mentally sound; be wealthy or honorable; get married, have children, make friends and what type, or travel widely; and what the individual will do as an occupation or for the community, and how he or she might die.

We will discuss each of these subjects briefly, telling you how to interrogate the natal chart so as to come up with answers to these most common questions. Casting lots or adding up strings of numerals—don't bother. Those are divination methods even those who use them cannot explain. We astrologers will concentrate on what we are able to predict using planetary aspects we can see and measure, and the planets' natural qualities and known effects.

First, let's talk about what's common to all charts, and what applies in all cases, and get that issue taken care of.

To answer a question or make a prediction, first look in the completed birth chart and determine its ruling planet by using the five criteria listed in the previous chapter; but in case you forgot, here they are again:

- whether a planet was in trine aspect to the ascendant degree
- whether a planet is exalted within its zodiac sign
- which house that planet occupies
- what "term" the planet belongs to in the house it occupies
- and its phase or aspect in relation to the planet that dominates the locale.

Then look at the area or house in the chart that best represents the subject in question. Sometimes a planet rather than a house will best represent the inquiry.

Notice that I said "area or house," and there is a difference. By "areas" of the chart I mean the four angles: ascendant, midheaven, descendant, and nadir. By "house" I mean one of the 12 sectors of the horoscope chart.

Here are the 12 astrological "houses" in a chart, and the events and conditions they rule:

[*Ptolemy did not write a list like the following one. He prioritized angles and aspects over houses in a chart, yet also used the 12 houses quite actively. These keywords frequently used to characterize each of the 12 houses seem modern, but they were drawn from Ptolemy's references to them.*]

House 1: physical self, vitality, drive, self-estimation, and what's most important to the self

House 2: money, wealth and values

House 3: siblings, neighbors, short trips, and communications

House 4: the person's foundation or home; the family home and the parent who ruled the home; heritage

House 5: creative capacity and activity, and children

House 6: health, work, service, and underlings

House 7: partners and mates

House 8: mysteries of the flesh: attraction, sexual relations, marriage, dangers, death and inheritance

House 9: education, politics, religion, philosophy, and journeys abroad

House 10: public or worldly activity and reputation, career, and the parent who was less often at home

House 11: associates, agreements, community, and friends; one's "tribe"

House 12: mysteries of spirit: emotions, faith, occult powers, troubles, self-undoing, and what is hidden or unexpressed

[*Returning to Ptolemy's text.*] Your goal is to identify the planet that rules the particular question you were asked. Here are two practical examples of how to do that:

Example 1: To answer a question about the individual's occupation, or public or worldly status, look at the birth chart's midheaven point (cusp of House 9 and House 10). Now consider, and seek your answer through this process:

- Which zodiac sign is on the midheaven?
- Which zodiac sign is rising?
- Are there planets in either of those zodiac signs? Which planets?
- Are those planets rising, or, if near the midheaven, are they past the midheaven and on their way to setting?
- Which planet governs the locale being asked about?
- Is there, among these planets, one that stands out by making any of the five basic aspects—conjunction, sextile, square, trine, and opposition—to other planets?
- If so, which planets make those aspects, what aspects do they make, and how many? The planet making the most aspects is the question's planetary ruler.

Example 2: To answer a question about events in the life of the individual's father, look at the birth chart's Sun, which among other things represents the male parent.

- Which zodiac sign is the Sun in?
- Look for aspects between the Sun and the other planets in the chart—again seeking out the five basic aspects: conjunction, sextile, square, trine, and opposition. Pay particular attention to any aspects with the planet that happens to rule the locale.
- The planet making the most aspects is the question's planetary ruler.
- If two or three planets make aspects, the one with the most aspects is the ruler. While deciding what your prediction should say, consider the nature of the ruling planet, the sign it is in, and the locale.
- The predicted event will be momentous if the ruling planet is powerfully placed and rising toward the midheaven; less so if the ruling planet is weak or has passed the midheaven and is on its way to the descendant. Then consider, looking at planetary positions:
- Is the birth chart's ruling planet "exalted" or "at home" and strong in the sign it is currently in, or is it in a sign or house that weakens it?

- Is the natal chart's ruling planet moving forward, or is it stationing or retrograding?

- Does the natal chart's ruling planet happen to sit at one of the four angles (ascendant, midheaven, descendant, or nadir) or, alternatively, in the house that "follows" the angle [*counterclockwise*] (Houses 1, 4, 7, or 10)? If the ruling planet is positioned in one of those places, the planet's power is on the increase.

- Is the natal chart's ruling planet in House 2, 5, 8, or 11? Then the planet's powers are "culminating," meaning its strength is at its peak.

- If, in the natal horoscope, the ruling planet is in House 3, 6, 9 or 12, the planet is said to be declining or separating from the angle, and its influence is less.

- The planet is weak if it it currently occupies a sign or house unrelated to it, is occidental, or in retrograde motion.

- To find out when the ruling planet's influence will be felt, look at the chart's four quadrants and find the ruling planet's position within them. Find out:

- Is the ruling planet at one of the four angles? Then the event will happen soon and the planet's influence will be strongest at its beginning.

- If the ruling planet rises before the Sun and occupies the chart's upper left quadrant, this also means the event will happen soon and the planet's influence will be strongest at the beginning.

- Does the ruling planet rise after the Sun and the ascendant? Then this event will take some time to unfold.

- Is the ruling planet setting, or is it in House 2, 5, 8, or 11? The event will not happen for a long time.

3.4. About the Parents and Planetary "Attendants"

The Sun and Saturn are naturally associated with fathers, and the Moon and Venus with mothers. The aspects these planets make to each other, and to stars or the angles, will tell us about the child's father and mother.

The Sun and Moon in a natal chart can show us whether the child will grow up rich. The parents will be rich and brilliantly so if the child has favorable planets "attending" on his or her Sun and Moon—"attending" meaning occupying the same houses as the Sun or Moon, or the houses following. Wealth is even more likely when the Sun is "attended" by favorable planets of the same sect, meaning they are serving as morning stars, and the Moon is "attended" by favorable planets serving as evening stars. Favorable "attendant" planets surrounding and following either Saturn or Venus show whether the parents' wealth comes from the father's or mother's side.

If the Sun and Moon, and especially Saturn and Venus, have no such attendants or are unfavorably positioned, the child has parents in humble or difficult circumstances. If the Sun and Moon have unfavorable planets "attending," such as Mars attending on the Sun or Saturn on the Moon, the parents' fortunes are moderate, or they fluctuate, but they are never wealthy.

The parents will be very happy together if both Saturn and Venus can be called "oriental" and are in their proper "faces" [*See Book One, chapter 23*], or if they are at the angles.

The natal Part of Fortune (to be explained in Book Three's chapter 10), positioned near the Sun or Moon and in company with favorable planets, means children's parental inheritance will be substantial. If the Part of Fortune is among any unfavorable planets attending on the Sun and Moon, or if there are no planetary attendants on the Sun or Moon, the inheritance will be disappointing or cause trouble among the heirs.

How long will the parents live? If Jupiter or Venus have any aspects to the Sun, or Saturn makes a conjunction, sextile, or trine to the Sun, the father will probably live long—if the Sun and Saturn themselves are in strong and favorable positions. If not, the father's life might not be short, but we cannot confirm that it will be long.

Indicators in the offspring's natal chart that his or her father might be sickly:

- if Mars is closer to the midheaven than the Sun is.
- if Mars closely follows the Sun or Saturn.
- if Saturn squares or opposes the Sun and those planets are in houses 3, 6, 9 and 12, the "cadent" houses.
- if Saturn and the Sun are on the ascendant and the midheaven angles.
- if Saturn and the Sun are on the descendant and the nadir.
- if Saturn and the Sun are both unfavorably positioned and in unfavorable aspect to each other.

The father is likely to die suddenly, or suffer injury to his face or eyes, if the child's natal Mars squares or opposes the child's natal Sun. If Mars squares or opposes Saturn, the father might have fatal seizures, fevers, infections, swelling, and wounds.

- The mother will live long if in the offspring's natal chart:
- Jupiter makes any aspect whatsoever to the Moon and to Venus
- the Sun is aspected, in any way, with the Moon or Venus
- the Moon is in conjunction, sextile, or trine with Venus.
- The mother is likely to be short-lived or sickly if:
- the houses preceding the Moon or Venus contain the planet Mars.
- Mars squares, opposes, or otherwise aspects the Moon or Venus. If it's a waxing Moon, she might die or go blind suddenly. If the Moon is waning, she might die after an abortion, or of cutting and cauterizing.

- Saturn squares the Moon. If the Moon is to the east of Saturn, the mother dies of chills and fever; if west of Saturn, of uterine disease or cancer.
- Saturn squares Venus. This causes death by fever or mysterious diseases.

Predicting specific diseases or causes of death requires that you take into account the zodiac signs you find these planets in, because in their qualities we can find the cause of the illness. The Sun and Venus are particularly important to your prediction if they are above the chart's horizon, and Saturn and the Moon if they are below the horizon.

To find out even more about the parents, make individual charts for each of them, this way: Use the degree of the child's natal Sun for the father, or the Moon for the mother, as the ascendant of the child's horoscope chart. Treat that chart as if it were the father's or the mother's natal chart. The houses and planetary rulerships of those charts might differ from those ruling the child's natal chart.

Also consider the planets ruling the locale the client is asking about. If those planets have no significant relationship to the planets most prominent in the client's natal chart, their influence will be weak and the event won't happen soon. And in that case, the ruling planet won't reveal the event's cause, either. For that, look for the planets that dominate the Sun and the angles.

Planets in the eastern quadrants indicate events that will happen sooner; those in western quadrants, later.

All this information, when successfully compiled, goes into making your predictions about your clients' parents.

3.5. About Brothers and Sisters

Predicting the number of a newborn's siblings cannot be done with one glance at the chart. Understand that some details, such as the exact number of siblings and their traits, are simply not discoverable. Treat the subject of siblings more generally.

When the question is about siblings related by blood, look at the zodiac signs which contain Venus by day and the Moon by night. Those signs and the ones following hold clues about the mother's children. Favorable planets located there mean many siblings. If those signs are simple [*no definition of "simple" is given in Book One, chapter 11, where the signs are categorized, or anywhere in* Tetrabiblos; *possibly "solid" is meant. The solid signs are Taurus, Leo, Scorpio, and Aquarius*] or bicorporeal (Gemini, Virgo, Sagittarius, and Pisces) the number of planets in those signs will equal the number of siblings.

But if the planets in those signs are unfavorable planets, or unfavorable planets oppose the favorable ones, expect few or no siblings. This is especially true if an unfavorable planet is in conjunction with or opposes the Sun. If the oppositions are on the angles, especially the ascendant and descendant, and if Saturn is also near the ascendant, the child represented will be the firstborn, or the first child to survive. If Mars is near the ascendant, siblings might be few because they don't survive.

Unfavorable planets positioned so that they seem to overpower the favorable ones are indicators that the siblings might not live for long. That is also true if the unfavorable planets rise after the favorable ones.

If the planets that indicate siblings are in a favorable aspect to the ascendant, the siblings will become esteemed adults. If not, the siblings will be ordinary.

To predict the genders of the siblings, focus your attention on two of the chart's quadrants: the quadrant from ascendant to the midheaven, and the quadrant from the descendant to the nadir. Then count the "male" planets and the "female" planets in those quadrants. Those farthest to the east will be born first, and the others later.

The question about the mother and siblings, depending on what that question specifically is, belongs to a particular house of the 12, and that house has a planetary ruler. Find it, and if that particular planet favorably aspects the planets that symbolize brothers and sisters, sibling relationships will be close and friendly. If not, and especially if that ruling planet opposes the sibling planets, expect the siblings to treat each other as enemies.

As with parents, to find out more about the siblings, use the degree of the planet that represents a certain sibling as the ascendant point of the subject's natal chart.

3.6. Predicting a Baby's Gender

The gender of the unborn cannot be determined by a single astrological factor. You have to use the whole chart, preferably a conception chart. But if you do not have one of those, set up a birth chart. [*Ptolemy does not explain how to set up a birth chart for those not yet born.*]

From the chart's Sun, Moon, ascendant, and the planets in aspect to them, we note particular tendencies toward the masculine or feminine. From these we "infer" that the unborn child is male or female.

It is essential when addressing this question to find out which planets rule the zodiac signs holding the Sun, Moon, and ascendant, and see how those planets relate to each other in the chart.

If the planetary aspects involving the Sun, Moon, and ascendant involve mostly masculine planets and masculine zodiac signs, and occupy the quadrants from the ascendant to the midheaven or the descendant to the nadir, expect a boy. If feminine and in the other quadrants, and there are other "feminine" indicators, expect a girl. If you don't recall which planets or zodiac signs are masculine and which are feminine, see Book One, chapters 6 and 12.

3.7. Predicting Twins or Multiple Births

Consult the Sun, Moon and ascendant as to whether twins, triplets, or more babies will be born. Note the houses the Sun, Moon, and ascendant are in, and the zodiac signs that happen to govern these houses, because the houses and the signs are especially important when answering this question.

If the Sun, Moon and ascendant happen to be in three separate houses, and those houses are all in harmonious aspect and furthermore governed by the bicorporeal zodiac signs Gemini, Virgo, Sagittarius and Pisces, and, in addition, most of the planets that rule them are in those bicorporeal zodiac signs, a multiple birth is likely. If pairs or groups of planets are in bicorporeal signs and all the aspects are favorable, that's an even stronger indicator of a multiple birth.

To foretell how many babies will be born, determine the planet that rules the chart. That would be the planet that makes the most aspects to the Sun, Moon, and ascendant. This planet and its placement are keys to the genders of the babies.

If all else in the chart signals a multiple birth and the Sun and Moon are at the midheaven, it's almost always twins and might be triplets.

Expect an all-male set of triplets if Saturn, Jupiter, and Mars are favorably configured with the Sun, Moon, and midheaven, and all are in the bicorporeal zodiac signs.

Expect an all-female set of triplets when Venus, the Moon, and Mercury (if Mercury's position renders that normally neutral planet feminine) are favorably configured with the Sun, Moon and ascendant, and all are in the bicorporeal zodiac signs.

Expect two boys and a girl when Saturn, Jupiter, and Venus are favorably configured with the Sun, Moon, and ascendant, and two girls and a boy if Venus, the Moon, and Mars are configured like that.

Often, in multiple births the babies are premature or have serious birth defects. Such births occur under unusual astral conditions.

3.8. Birth Defects

Regarding the chances that a baby will have serious birth defects, look at the Sun and Moon. Suspect birth defects if the Sun and Moon are far as possible from the ascendant or entirely unrelated to it, and if both Saturn and Mars are between the ascendant and midheaven or the midheaven and the descendant. If you see those factors, seek more information to confirm it. Find the degree of the last new Moon or full Moon preceding the birth. If this degree in no way relates to the chart's ascendant, or the Moon, or the place of birth, that's ominous.

If the Sun and Moon are unrelated in any way to the full or new Moon's planetary ruler, and that Sun and Moon happen to be in the zodiac signs which are shaped like animals, and both Saturn or Mars are between that Sun and Moon, expect birth defects so severe the fetus is hard to recognize as human.

If Jupiter and Venus are between that Sun and Moon, expect an intersex or hermaphroditic baby. If along with Jupiter and Venus, Mercury is between the Sun and Moon, it is possible that the baby, even with defects, will be a prophet and earn money from this talent. If Mercury is alone between the Sun and Moon, sometimes the baby is born deaf or will be toothless, but he or she will be intelligent and cunning.

3.9. Babies That Die, are Given Up, or Abandoned

For predicting whether the baby will survive its first year and be raised by its biological parents, the usual "length of life" calculation does not apply. That calculation applies only to those who survive past the first year, also called one solar cycle.

The cosmic influences that allow you to predict that a baby will never grow up are complicated and must be judged with the greatest care:

The Sun or Moon must be on one of the angles, and

an unfavorable planet must be in conjunction with or opposing the Sun or Moon—and

this opposition must be exact in both degree and declination.

Also, the chart must show that no favorable planets play any part in this arrangement.

If the Sun or Moon are very closely followed by both Saturn and Mars, or Saturn or Mars oppose them exactly, these unfavorable planets emit rays that afflict either the Sun or Moon, or both, and the baby will be stillborn or die soon after birth. The same is true if the Sun and Moon are on the chart's angles and one or both unfavorable planets form an isosceles triangle with the Sun and Moon.

If there happen to be favorable planets separating from recent conjunctions with the afflicted Sun or Moon, the baby will live for a while, and here is how to tell how long that will be. It'll be months, days, or hours—any one of those three—equal to the number of degrees between the Sun or Moon and the nearest unfavorable planetary "rays" [*usually meaning proximity to, or oppositions or squares from, Saturn or Mars*]. Which of those three units of time, months, days or hours, should you use? The unit of time will be in proportion to how badly the Sun and Moon are afflicted and the exactness of the angle and declination of the nearest unfavorable planet.

Abandoned babies will be adopted and raised if the unfavorable planets are separating from recent conjunctions with the afflicted Sun or Moon, and favorable planets are right behind them. If the unfavorable rays are too close, the adopted baby will grow up unhappy or perhaps abused. But when the favorable planets are closer, the adopted baby will thrive.

An abandoned baby will be returned to and raised by its own parents if, under all these conditions, a favorable planet is rising while an unfavorable one sets.

All of the above is true for multiple births as well.

3.10. Figuring the Potential Lifespan

Second in importance to the birth is the lifespan, because predicting character traits and life events is a waste of time if the life will not be lived. But predicting a lifespan is not simple or easy. I present the method that most aligns with reason and nature.

Ruling planets will figure strongly in what follows.

We begin measuring a lifespan from a natal chart by establishing a point on the ecliptic. The person's lifespan, as granted at birth, is a journey from this point on the ecliptic to another.

This journey always meets with obstacles; those are the crisis points in life. Eventually there is a point along the ecliptic at which the life energy runs out.

In figuring lifespans, the initial, life-giving point or planet is called the Hyleg. The planet that measures out our years is called the Alcoccoden. The planets or planet, or specific points in the chart that threaten to end a life are called anaretas, and there is always more than one Anareta.

[*Please understand that:*

- *When Ptolemy's astrology calculates a person's lifespan, it's the potential length of life—the amount of life force the universe has portioned out to that particular being at birth. Accidents, disasters, war, violence, or risky behavior can take a person's life before his or her life force runs out. Ptolemy said this in Book One.*

- *Estimates of lifespan do not include accidental deaths, such as falling off a cliff. An astrological lifespan is lived to its end only if there are no such accidents and if the person meets with no lethal earthly phenomena such as falling boulders or volcanic eruptions. Triggered solely by nature, such events are not astrologically predictable. Ptolemy explains this in Book One.*]

As we stated in the previous chapter, we do not do lifespan inquiries for children less than one year old. They have not yet accumulated enough time on Earth to form a basis for the inquiry.

To begin to figure the potential length of life, you have ten elements in the natal chart to look at and consider: the seven planets, plus the ascendant, the midheaven, and the Part of Fortune.

The ascendant in this type of inquiry is an area stretching from 5 degrees above the eastern horizon to 25 degrees beneath it. In lifespan calculation, for a planet to be called "ascendant," it must be within this 30-degree range.

The Part of Fortune, not a planet and not visible in the sky, is a point in a person's natal chart showing in what area of life he or she will be most fortunate. Everybody's chart has its own Part of Fortune, figured according to a standard formula.

Figuring the Part of Fortune

When figuring the Part of Fortune, it does not matter whether the birth occurred during daylight or at night.

The figuring is done in two steps:

1. Measure the number of degrees (maximum, 360 degrees) from the Sun to the Moon, following the zodiac in its normal [*counterclockwise*] order.

2. Measure this same number of degrees from the ascendant, following the zodiac in its normal order, and that leads you to the Part of Fortune point.

Like a planet, the Part of Fortune will be in one of the zodiac signs and one of the chart's houses, and can be interpreted accordingly. Unlike the planets, it has no traits beyond being an indicator of good fortune.

The Starting Point: The Hyleg

Have ready the natal chart, with its angles established, and have at hand the table of the essential planetary dignities:

Sign	*Home*	*Exaltation*	*Fall*
Aries	Mars	Sun	Saturn
Taurus	Venus	Moon	*None*
Gemini	Mercury	*None*	*None*
Cancer	Moon	Jupiter	Mars
Leo	Sun	*None*	*None*
Virgo	Mercury	Mercury	Venus
Libra	Venus	Saturn	Sun
Scorpio	Mars	*None*	Moon
Sagittarius	Jupiter	*None*	*None*
Capricorn	Saturn	Mars	Jupiter
Aquarius	Saturn	*None*	*None*
Pisces	Jupiter	Venus	Mercury

Which of the ten elements in the chart is strongest, and, if it's a tie, which has the most favorable planetary aspects? That planet or point is called, in Arabic, the Hyleg. It is the astrological Giver of Life, representing the emergent life force in the natal chart.

Ideally, the Hyleg should be placed, in order of preference, at the midheaven (on the cusp of Houses 9 and 10) or in House 10, 1, 11 [*Ptolemy refers to House 11 as "house of the good spirit"*], 7 [*referred to as "the occident"*] or 9 [*referred to as "the house of the god."*]. Notice the order of preference. At the midheaven the Hyleg is strongest. In House 10 the Hyleg's strength is far greater than if it were in House 9.

Planets in House 8 and and in House 12 [*Ptolemy refers to House 12 as "the house of the evil spirit"*] cannot serve as the Hyleg, ever. House 12 is fumy with Earth's moisture so the planets and stars there do not look like their true selves.

Houses beneath the horizon cannot be home to the Hyleg, except for the area within the ascendant zone.

If the Hyleg is not in one of the preferred houses, maybe the natal Sun or Moon is in one of those houses. If so, use that Sun or Moon point as the Hyleg point.

If neither the Sun nor the Moon are in those houses, then do this:

If the Sun was above the horizon at the birth:

Make a chart for the new Moon that most closely preceded the birth.

If the degree of that new Moon before the birth was in the natal chart's House 10, 1, 11, 7, or 9, use that degree as the natal Hyleg. If it is not in House 10, 1, 11, 7, or 9, then use the new Moon chart's Hyleg as the natal Hyleg. If all else fails, use the natal ascendant as the Hyleg.

If the Sun was below the horizon at birth:

If the new Moon before the birth was more recent than the full Moon, use the ascendant as the Hyleg. If the full Moon before the birth was more recent than the new Moon, use the Part of Fortune as the Hyleg, but only if it falls in Houses 1, 10, 11, 7, or 9.

If the individual was born during daylight hours, the best Hyleg to have, in order of preference, is the Sun, the Moon, the planet with the most essential dignities, and the ascendant. If the birth was at night, the best Hyleg is the Moon; then, in order of preference, the Sun; the planet with the most essential dignities related to the Moon; the point of the full Moon that preceded the birth; and then the Part of Fortune.

Next, look at the sign of the zodiac the Hyleg is in, and the planet that rules that sign.

The ruling planet of the Hyleg is called the Alcoccoden, and this planet is the time lord in charge of the individual's lifespan. [*Ptolemy gives here no further information about the Alcoccoden or how to use it. He does, however, describe how to find a planetary time lord in Book Four, chapter 11.*]

Then figure the anaretas. In any chart there is always more than one. The planet making the most and worst possible aspects to the Hyleg is probably an Anareta. It is most likely one of the unfavorable planets, Saturn or Mars. An Anareta can also be a particular degree.

In longevity calculation, the placements of Saturn and Mars afflict the planets or the zodiac signs not only when they are near or in them but when they are in opposition or in square aspect to them, or in the signs which "behold" the signs they occupy. The Sun, on the other hand, when in aspect, will neutralize just about anything, whether good or bad, with one exception: When the Moon is the Hyleg, the sign the Sun occupies is destructive for it.

When the planets and their placements both look bad, the outlook is gloomy. If only one of those looks bad, a crisis emerges but will pass.

Anaretas can be unfavorable planets or degrees in conjunction with, or making unfavorable aspects to, the natal ascendant, Sun, or Moon. Anaretas are crisis points that can threaten the life, such as episodes of serious illness. Only one degree in a natal chart is an Anareta always: the degree of the chart's descendant, because it opposes the ascendant, which is the lord of life.

Remember, do not estimate lifespans for infants under one year old. Other people will do that type of chart, but I recommend against it.

There are two ways to calculate lifespans. Both involve updates to the natal chart. One, to be used only if the Hyleg is between the ascendant and midheaven, is to keep the ascendant point, Hyleg and Alcoccoden where they are in the natal chart and move the natal planets ahead, through the normal order of the zodiac, counterclockwise, one degree for each year of life; then study how their new positions relate to the Hyleg and Alcoccoden. The other is to leave the natal planets where they are and move the ascendant point, clockwise, up toward the midheaven, one degree per each year of life, and, in step with it, move the Hyleg and Alcoccoden ahead by one degree, and that's the method I want to concentrate on.

[*Here begins the most controversial and confusing part of* Tetrabiblos. *Ptolemy's lifespan calculation method, and those of later astrologers such as Bonatti and Lilly who tried to simplify it, when tested today fail to provide consistent or accurate lifespan estimates. Some say because of advancements in medical care we can today outlive our given lifespan. Others say there's no point in lifespan predictions that don't account for accidents, acts of war or nature, epidemics, crimes, or self-harm. Multiple anaretas provide multiple possible threatening occasions, but nothing definite; people can and have survived the harshest anaretas. Others say Ptolemy befogged his prose in this chapter to discourage astrologers from presenting with confidence predictions likely to be both inaccurate and terrifying. All can agree with 16th-century astrologer Argoli that Ptolemy's instructions regarding lifespan calculation have "very poor clarity."*

Western astrologers today as a matter of ethics agree not to attempt to predict a living person's lifespan because, despite a few claims to the contrary, no method has been discovered that really works, or else actuaries and physicians would be using it—and such a prediction would worry the client.

A free online calculator you can set to Ptolemy's formula or William Lilly's is at http://af.cpptea.com/astrofox.php?dat=5 (retrieved 3 June 2017).

Ptolemy's preferred lifespan estimate formula is based on a common astrological predictive technique called Primary Directions.

The natal chart is a "snapshot" of the sky at the time and place of a birth. A natal chart never changes. But after the snapshot, the day marches on, and from Earth's point of view the stars, planets, and constellations seem to rise, drift westward, and then set, continually, as if the heavens were turning. But the heavens do not turn; the Earth turns, completing one full rotation on its axis in a little under 24 hours. After one rotation the stars and planets seem to return to their original places, but only briefly. They forever keep moving westward, in what we call "diurnal motion," at the measured pace of about 1 degree every 4 minutes, or 15 degrees per hour.

Ptolemy's Hyleg point and subsequently the Alcoccoden point are calculated using a natal chart. A natal chart stays forever as it is, like the numerals on a clock face. But like a clock's minute hand, instead of being frozen in place the Hyleg point is allowed to keep pace with the Earth's diurnal motion.

The Hyleg and the Alcoccoden points, because they move, will therefore make new contacts with the natal chart's planets, angles and other points of interest at predictable times in the future. Each degree between Hyleg or Alcoccoden and the next Anareta counts as one year. Astrologers can see these contacts coming and, theoretically, could then tell clients, "In X number of years, look out for a serious threat to your life."

That's a highly simplified outline of how the formula is supposed to work. As Ptolemy explains in his harrowing example, every case requires mathematical corrections because the ecliptic, the path of the zodiac signs and planets, is not the same as the celestial equator but rather at a 23.5-degree angle to it. The birth locale's latitude too must be factored in, and, for precision, also the fact that Earth's rotation takes a fraction less than 24 hours. Ptolemy also mentioned that differing declinations can defuse what appear to be showdown planetary conjunctions. But most crucially, Primary Directions are dependent on natal charts based on seriously accurate birth times. When a natal chart is founded on a birth time that happens to be four minutes off from the actual birth time, a prediction using primary directions will be "off" by one whole year.

Now we enter the realm of subjectivity. Identifying the truly dangerous aspects that create anaretas is a judgement call, and that is where the system, as a symbolic science, breaks down. According to Ptolemy, anaretic points are determined by the planets involved and their aspects and "rays," the influences of the natal houses, planetary dignities and debilities, the chart's Alcoccoden or time lord, angles and more. Someone has to collate, weigh, and judge all these, and in the matter of lifespan the chances of accuracy are exceptionally small and the stakes exceptionally high.

Ptolemy has further mitigating advice for astrologers who attempt to calculate the length of a life:

- *Examine every possible factor before designating an Anareta.*
- *The natal chart's descendant degree is always a formidable Anareta.*
- *People can survive anaretas.*
- *Only badly afflicted anaretas are dangerous; contacts with anaretas not badly afflicted might pass without incident.*
- *A badly afflicted Sun can be an Anareta if no favorable planet "rescues" it.*
- *Saturn and Mars are the crisis planets and can threaten life when they square or oppose the natal Hyleg or Alcoccoden. Saturn and Mars might cause harm even when they make trine or sextile aspects, which are normally interpreted as favorable.*
- *Contacts with favorable planets or points preserve the life force; contacts with unfavorable planets diminish or put pressure on the life force.*
- *The planet Mercury can be favorable or unfavorable depending on the planet it is closest to.*
- *Anaretas might be neutralized if they are within 12 degrees of natal Jupiter or 8 degrees of natal Venus.*

3.11. An Example of Lifespan Calculation

[This much simplified version is intended to give readers a basic idea of how Ptolemy's longevity prediction method, today called Primary Directions, worked. Astrological software can swiftly and correctly

calculate primary directions, more popular as a predictive tool in Ptolemy's time than now. It is unfortunate that Ptolemy did not give detailed theoretical or practical instructions regarding the Alcoccoden, or planetary time lord, of the chart, or how to interpret it in relation to longevity. Medieval and Renaissance astrologers studied the Alcoccoden intensively but were unable to pin it to a formula that gave consistent results. To most modern astrologers, the centuries of effort poured into finding a lifespan formula are a historical curiosity.

1. Have a natal chart calculated and ready.

2. Find the Hyleg, or "giver of life" point according the method in the previous chapter. If you cannot find the Hyleg, use the birth chart's ascendant as the Hyleg. Determine the planetary ruler of the Hyleg and its point in the chart. This is the Alcoccoden, the "measurer" of life.

3. Keep the chart's planets as if frozen in place, but allow the ascendant to rise one degree for every year of life. For example, if the natal ascendant is 16 degrees, 18 minutes of Scorpio (rendered as 16 Scorpio 18), at the age of one year the chart's ascendant would be 17 degrees, 18 minutes of Scorpio (17 Scorpio 18). Wherever the Hyleg is, it also moves one degree west for every year of life, in step with the Alcoccoden. Remember, though, that while we do this the natal planets and angles do not move, although adjacent houses or zodiac signs might encase them.

4. Keeping your attention on the Hyleg point, move the ascendant up by another degree, and then another, and then another, counting each degree, looking for places the newly-situated Hyleg or Alcoccoden points, or both, make contact by aspect with a possibly threatening natal planet or point of interest such as the natal chart's descendant. Interpret this aspect in accordance with information in the previous chapter.

A word-for-word translation of Ptolemy's original text is found in Ptolemy: Tetrabiblos, *translated by F.E. Robbins, Harvard University Press, 1940.*

Returning to Ptolemy's text.]

3.12. Looks and Temperament

The body is formed as it attracts and accumulates more of the qualities of its beginning, and similarly some time must pass before the soul's quality is evident. So we will consider first the appearance and character of the individual's body. The body's quality at birth might be altered by later life events.

To form a prediction about the body, look at the chart's ascendant and the planets there, and if there are no planets, look at:

- the planet that rules the ascendant, and
- any fixed stars rising at the time of birth, and
- especially the position of the Moon.

These things together—ascendant, its planetary ruler, fixed stars and the Moon—are the basis of the form the individual's body takes. The ruling planets are the most important factors, though.

How Ruling Planets Shape a Person's Looks

If Saturn rules and is between the eastern horizon and meridian [*rising*], the person will be dark-skinned, dark-haired, curly-haired, hairy, vigorous, of average height, with dark eyes of average size. His or her temperament will be like Saturn's: wet and cold.

If Saturn is post-meridian [*setting*], the body will be dark-skinned, black-eyed, and dark-haired also, but slender and short and graceful, with scanty body hair, and the temperament will be mostly cold and dry.

If Jupiter is rising, the body is light-skinned yet has good color, is tall and commanding, and the eyes are large and hair somewhat curled. The temperament is hot and moist.

If Jupiter is setting, the skin is pale, the hair straight and thin or receding, the body of average height, and the temperament is too moist.

Mars rising gives people rosy complexions and gray eyes, with thick wavy hair. These people are tall and vigorous and their temperament is warm and dry.

Mars setting gives people ruddy complexions and straight yellow hair, and scanty body hair. They are of average height, and the eyes are small. This temperament is definitely dry.

Venus rising or setting gives traits similar to Jupiter's, but the bodies given by Venus are well-proportioned and plump, feminine (even the men's), and voluptuous, with bright and beautiful eyes, as one would expect.

Mercury, when rising, makes people sallow, of average height, well-coordinated, with small eyes and wavy hair; their temperament is overly warm.

Mercury setting gives people light skin with no healthy glow although the cheeks might be reddish. The skin has an olive undertone. They might be extra thin, with bright, darting eyes. Their temperament is dry.

The Sun in aspect to any of these planets will intensify the body's good traits and sturdiness. The Moon, especially when separating from a planet or planetary aspect, provides slimmer and better-proportioned bodies, and the proportions are different depending on the phase of the natal moon. Moon phases are described in detail in Book One, chapter 8.

When the planets Venus and Mercury are morning stars, stature and stamina increase. If a morning-star planet is in direct motion, the body is less well-proportioned. If stationing and preparing to go retrograde, these planets grant a strong, muscular body. If in retrograde and stationing, preparing to go direct, the body is weak. If either Venus or Mercury is an evening star, the body is nondescript but able to withstand hardships.

The planets' placements in zodiac signs also influence the body's form and the soul's temperament. Planets in Aries through Gemini grant a nice complexion and nice eyes, a strong body and some height, and the temperament is moist and warm. People with planets in Cancer through Virgo are strong, large-eyed with curly hair, of medium stature and have better than average complexions. Their temperament is dry and warm. Planets in Libra through Sagittarius tend to make thin, sallow, sickly bodies, nonetheless with striking eyes and moderately curly hair, and their temperament is dry and cold. Planets in Capricorn through Pisces contribute darker skin, straight hair, medium height, scant body hair, good coordination, and their temperament is cold and moist.

Zodiac signs of human shape—Gemini, Virgo, Sagittarius, and Aquarius—and constellations that have human shapes improve the body's proportion and coordination. The other signs influence bodies so they might resemble the animals or objects that represent them, creating different proportions. For example, Leo, Virgo, and Sagittarius make limbs larger; Pisces, Capricorn, and Cancer make them smaller. Aries, Taurus, and Leo favor the body's upper half over the lower, which could be weak. Sagittarius, Scorpio, and Gemini add slenderness with robust hind parts. Virgo, Libra, and Sagittarius contribute grace. Scorpio, Pisces, and Taurus bring about disproportionate bodies and poor coordination.

By combining all the relevant astrological factors we can make a guess about the subject's body and temperament.

3.13. About Sicknesses and Injuries

Get a general idea about a person's bodily sicknesses and injuries from looking at the natal chart's ascendant and descendant, most especially the descendant and the zodiac sign preceding it. That sign is disjunct (five signs away from) the sign of the ascendant. That would be House 6 on the chart. Then look for Saturn and Mars in the chart and see what aspects they make to these houses. To be specific:

Expect diseases and injuries if Saturn and/or Mars are on the ascendant or descendant, are square to the ascendant or descendant, or oppose them. This is especially true if the Sun or Moon is in House 1 but not within orb of conjunction with the ascendant point, or either luminary is in House 7 without being within conjunction of the descendant point.

If Saturn or Mars is rising before the Sun or Moon, or rising just after them and on an angle, use the zodiac signs and natures of the afflicting or afflicted planet as a clue to the disease.

Each zodiac sign rules a part of the body, and the sign on the afflicted ascendant or descendant allows you to predict the type of illness or injury afflicting that part of the body. Details such as the cause of the illness or injury can be provided by the nature of the planet or planets in aspect to them.

Here we list planets along with the body parts and functions they rule:

- Saturn: right ear, spleen, bladder, phlegm, bones
- Jupiter: skin and the sense of touch, lungs, arteries, semen
- Mars: left ear, kidneys, veins, genitals

- Venus: the sense of smell, skin, the liver
- Mercury: the brain, speech and thought, the tongue, bile, and buttocks
- Moon: the sense of taste, ability to swallow, stomach, belly, womb, and the body's left side
- Sun: eyesight, brain, heart, sinews, and the body's right side

Injuries heal, but diseases persist; that's the difference between them. Generally, when Saturn and Mars are in the east there are injuries, and when they are in the west and setting, diseases attack suddenly or are chronic.

Blindness in one eye can be furthered by:

- the Moon on the ascendant, descendant, or full—meaning it will have some relationship to the Sun—but especially when the Moon has some kind of contact with the Sun and is in conjunction with the star clusters in Cancer (the Beehive), Taurus (the Pleiades), Sagittarius (at its arrow's point), Scorpio (in its stinger), Leo (in the vicinity of the Lion's tail), or Aquarius (in his water pitcher).
- the waning Moon being on one of the four angles, and Mars and Saturn rising and approaching it are also angular and rise before the Sun.
- Causes of blindness in both eyes:
- when Mars and Saturn, both at once, are in the same sign or in opposition to the Sun and Moon. Mars in particular brings about blindness by violence, weapons, or burning.
- If Mercury is in aspect, blindness may be caused by sporting accidents or criminal attack.
- Saturn, because it's moist, can fog the vision, create pressure in the eye (glaucoma) and trigger other such conditions having to do with fluids.
- Reproductive harm including sterility, miscarriages, premature birth, babies born with abnormal genitalia, and injuries to the male genitalia can occur when:
- Venus is on the angles, particularly the descendant, and especially when it is joined with Saturn or is in unfavorable aspect to Saturn, or Venus and Saturn have exchanged houses. This is particularly true if the planets involved are in Cancer, Virgo, or Capricorn.
- The Moon is rising in conjunction with Mars, or it is involved in aspects with both Saturn and Mercury, with Mars rising before the Moon or in opposition to it. The effect is stronger when the Sun is also involved in the aspect, along with Venus made masculine, if the Moon is waning, and especially if the signs Aries, Leo, Scorpio, Capricorn and Aquarius are involved.

The person can be tongue-tied or lisping when Saturn and Mercury are joined with the Sun at the angles, particularly if Mercury is setting and both planets are in aspect with the Moon. The presence of Mars along with them might loosen the tongue.

The person can be lame or hunchbacked if the Sun and Moon, together or in opposition, are approaching Saturn or Mars when those planets are on the angles. If the Moon is at one of its nodes or squaring its nodes, or if the signs Aries, Taurus, Cancer, Scorpio, or Capricorn are involved, the handicap or paralysis is congenital. If Saturn and Mars are joined with the Sun and Moon at the midheaven, the handicap is the result of injury.

Skin diseases such as leprosy tend to manifest when the Moon is in the signs of solstices and equinoxes.

Diseases the unfavorable planets are likely to cause, each in accord with the planet's nature:

Saturn: rheumatism, weakness, jaundice, dysentery, coughing up phlegm, colic, elephantiasis; and Saturn in addition afflicts females with uterine diseases.

Mars: Men spit blood, have lung problems, depression, itchy skin, scurvy, fistulas, hemorrhoids, ulcers or tumors. Women are inclined to miscarry or have other female problems.

Mercury in aspect with Saturn keeps the illness dragging on, and among its effects are fluid retention in the chest, throat, and stomach. Mercury in aspect with Mars, whose nature is dry, brings sore or ulcerated eyes, psoriasis, abscesses, skin eruptions, black bile, insanity, or epilepsy.

The zodiac signs involved can affect the kind of disease that might erupt: Cancer, Capricorn and Pisces are related to skin diseases, fistulas, and elephantiasis, and Gemini and Sagittarius to seizures. When the planets involved are in the final degrees of a sign, they cause diseases of the extremities, such as gout or leg ulcers.

Chances of recovery increase if favorable planets make aspects to disease-causing planetary configurations, and the more such planets, the better. Jupiter mitigates disease or allows it to be successfully hidden. Mercury signifies good doctors and medications. Venus's presence means divine healing is at work, and maybe the scars, blemishes or irregularities will be viewed as attractive. If Saturn is near Venus, the person will not be able to hide the disease, but it is curable. If Mercury is near Venus, the person's disease or injury might result in personal or financial gains.

3.14. The Quality of the Character

Mercury and the Moon govern character. Mercury represents the person's mind, and the Moon, his or her emotional and instinctual qualities. But trying to find out about someone's character is not at all simple, because a person's character is a vast, living, active entity and does so much.

First, some useful generalizations:

Mercury and the Moon are the first places to look when judging character. Look also at their aspects to the Sun and the angles. The zodiac signs involved can strongly influence the character. Planetary aspects and their qualities, and each of the planets and their particular qualities, affect a person's character.

Here's a list of the personal traits the zodiac signs generate in the character or soul:

Cardinal Signs (Aries, Cancer, Libra, Capricorn): social, political, serving the people, a desire for excitement and personal glory, inquisitive, secretive, noble, inventive, active, and devoted to their faith. They make good astrologers and diviners.

Mutable or Bicorporeal Signs (Gemini, Virgo, Sagittarius, Pisces): changeable, versatile, complex, hard to understand, jokey or fickle, lazy, fun-seeking, fond of music, covetous, and amorous.

Fixed or Solid Signs (Taurus, Leo, Scorpio, Aquarius): fair, firm to the point of hard-heartedness, intelligent, ambitious, grasping, persistent, industrious, patient, immune to flattery, self-controlled, curmudgeonly, begrudging, and inflexible.

When looking at an individual's horoscope, if you see planetary placements that are in exaltation or otherwise favorably placed the person will be open-minded, simple, strong, noble, perceptive and friendly. Planetary stations and culminations at the ascendant or in the upper left and lower right quadrants of the chart make these people intelligent, friendly, patient, calculating, goal-oriented, determined, critical, vengeful, hard to deceive, yet generous and understanding. Planets that are setting and at the same time in direct motion (as opposed to retrograde) encourage the traits of emotional and physical weakness, including cowardice, being slothful in body and mind, bullying, and unwilling to work.

Planets in the western half of the chart, and particularly at the nadir, make a person wise, noble, a spiritual seeker and reader of dreams and omens. Philosophical, and a fine craftsman when he or she feels like it, this person has a poor memory and can lazily try to get away with sloppy work. This is particularly true if Mercury and Venus set during the daylight hours and rise at night.

When Mercury and the Moon are the planetary governors of the soul and comfortably and favorably placed in their zodiac signs, houses and sects, expect the soul's character to be open and direct, secure and honest, and that this person will function well. It's even better if in the horoscope some planets, especially Mercury and the Moon, are in mutual reception [*in each other's zodiacal "home" sign or sign of exaltation*], and if the Moon is approaching conjunction with a favorable planet or has just passed the point of that conjunction.

If Mercury and the Moon aren't happily placed, these people's souls are ineffective, troubled, disorderly, and do not function as they should.

I told you that predicting and reading a person's soul are not easy tasks. Unfavorable planets and aspects in a chart might overpower a favorably placed Moon and Mercury. A powerfully placed Saturn or Mars can create souls mean and unjust. Yet this soul can stay direct and very open about, for example, wanting to kill or hurt somebody, and believes that this is honorable behavior. If these planets are overcome by those of the opposite sect, this helps curb their aggression and meaner impulses.

It's also possible that a soul with a very favorably placed Moon and Mercury might be kindly and happy and benefit by his or her goodness, but if Saturn or Mars overwhelms the chart, good intentions are treated contemptuously, or he or she is considered a pushover.

So the above is most of what you need to know about judging character in general. Now we address the particulars.

First, identify the planet that dominates the soul.

A planet effectively dominates, if, in the natal chart, several of these conditions are met:

the planet is on an angle, especially the midheaven

it is in a trine or sextile aspect to one of the angles

it is not in a disjunct sign

it is in a "solid" zodiac sign (Taurus, Leo, Scorpio, Aquarius)

it is in a quadrant the same gender as itself

it is in a zodiac sign the same gender as itself

it is in its governing sign or house

it is exalted in the zodiac sign it is in

it is in one of the terms assigned to it (for "terms," see Book One, chapter 21).

Aspects of Saturn

If Saturn alone rules the chart and is more powerful than Mercury and the Moon, the person has good health habits, thinks deeply, follows a strict moral code, is purposeful, works hard, loves property and money perhaps too much, and can be violent, dictatorial, and punitive.

Saturn poorly aspected in a chart, without dignity, makes a person petty, mean, sleazy, cowardly, manipulative, shameless, superstitious, gloomy, a busybody, sentimental, a schemer against his or her own friends, and a slob about self-care.

If Saturn makes a favorable aspect to Jupiter, and Jupiter is itself well-placed in the horoscope, the person is generous, wise, patient, respectful, has critical intelligence, is a loyal friend, thoughtful, and philosophical. If conditions are the opposite, the person is crass, superstitious, a hypochondriac who talks endlessly about aches and pains, feels that children are a burden, is hard-boiled, hypocritical, mean and unapproachable, yet easily manipulated.

A well-placed Saturn making a strong aspect to a well-placed Mars creates assertive personalities who work hard but are rough-edged, pitiless, tyrannical, angry with everyone, and argumentative. Their behavior and especially their speech are outspoken, rude, and careless. They know how to stir up a mob. Very practical people, they manage to outmaneuver their competition and are remarkably successful at achieving their goals.

A badly placed Saturn in aspect to a badly placed Mars creates murderers, robbers and thieves, slavishness, cynicism, heartlessness, and craftiness applied to evil deeds.

A well-placed Saturn in aspect to a well-placed Venus creates cautious, shrewd people who can't appreciate beauty. Their opinions are fixed, especially on the topics of women or religious or spiritual beliefs, and they are easily offended. They'll whine that the old days were better than now. Unfriendly, often preferring to be without any friends, they are nonetheless faithful to their spouses and very jealous.

A poorly-placed Saturn in aspect to a poorly-placed Venus creates substance addicts, sex fiends with no morals or taboos, people who hurt and lie to everyone including their spouses and kin, and are judgmental and cynical with passive-aggressive personalities. They too hate anything beautiful or noble, use foul language, and have only contempt for religion.

A well-placed Saturn in favorable aspect to Mercury grants an inquisitive mind. These are smart and worldly businesspeople, medics, and mystics, but also con artists, forgers, teasers, and frauds. If the aspect to Mercury is unfavorable, they behave as if there's no tomorrow, know the price of everything but the value of nothing, are cynical about everyone, will say anything no matter how baseless or outrageous, and betray or steal even from their relatives. Eventually their luck runs out.

Aspects of Jupiter

If Jupiter alone is the dominant planet in the chart, the person has role-model and leadership qualities. Generous, kind, civil, easy to talk with, modest, warmhearted and open-minded, they love debates, art, and good clean fun. With a badly placed Jupiter, the person has the opposite traits. Their poor judgement leads to conceit, cowardice, and spendthrift behavior. Instead of loving what is beautiful, they love what is pleasurable and don't care what happens to others.

Jupiter favorably aspected with Mars makes soldiers and managers who are rough and critical yet vigorous, ambitious and effective. These people are restless, will plot and argue and want to be the boss. Yet they are generous, fair and successful. An unfavorable aspect from Jupiter to Mars creates exasperating characters who don't know what they want but are stubborn and defiant anyway. They might be unstable, gossipy, kooky, or "out to lunch," and think they know everything.

Jupiter in favorable aspect to Venus creates artists and art lovers with both charm and dignity, as well as competitive athletes. The men are gentlemen. These people are trustworthy and generous, donate to charities, and want to be recognized as good people. They accept only the best so they choose worthy friends and partners, and love their families. Jupiter in bad aspect to Venus creates lazy moochers and party people in love with themselves, who expect to be waited on, pile up expensive clothes and accessories, are effeminate and lecherous. Occult rituals and practices attract them. On the good side, they can be gracious and cheerful and will help troubled friends.

Jupiter in favorable aspect to Mercury makes gifted intellectuals such as mathematicians, poets, and leaders who want to benefit all humanity. Good-natured and generous, they are worthy advisers and confidantes, will take you seriously, have excellent manners they grew up with, are religious but don't flaunt it, and devoted to their families. They maintain their dignity under all conditions. Jupiter in unfavorable aspect to Mercury makes people well-informed but also fanatical, puritanical, and bitter. Their memories work well, and if they want to, they can be teachers. Or they can seem deranged.

Aspects of Mars

If Mars alone dominates the soul and the planet is favorably placed in the chart, we have powerful, headstrong, spirited, and active people with leadership qualities. They can also go over the top and become tyrants, loose cannons, and malcontents. Often they are attracted to things military. A badly placed governing Mars creates troublemakers and loudmouths often spoiling for a fight. They can be misanthropes, drunks, and spendthrifts and nothing is sacred to them.

If Mars is in favorable aspect to Venus, these souls are happy pleasure-lovers, gourmands, and property owners. They are sensible, enjoy the arts, and stay in step with fashion, but the men stay masculine. Sex is their weakness. Their very discreet affairs, often with young lovers, are perhaps bisexual, and they are very sexually jealous. If Mars and Venus aspect each other unfavorably, the people are grossly corrupt, totally shameless, treacherous in every way, and ignore authorities. They like luxuries, especially those they can wear, and have no problem seeking out sex with the married or under-aged, or relatives.

When Mars favors Mercury, we often see military officers and others who are active, resourceful, keenly observant, and rigidly hierarchical people. Mercury's influence has them thinking they are sly and know every trick in the book. They are loyal to their own kind, but only their own kind. Mars in unfavorable aspect to Mercury creates criminals and fraudsters with hair-trigger tempers, greedy villains, and slick and daring fake sorcerers and shamans.

Aspects of Venus

If the planet Venus by itself dominates a person's character and is positively placed, these are charming, well-spoken people, esthetes, dreamers, art and theater buffs. They disapprove of unseemly or nasty behavior and are careful not to be nasty themselves but to practice compassion and generosity. A badly placed governing Venus creates small-souled people: timid yet critical of others, effeminate, inconsequential, and lustful.

Venus in favorable aspect with Mercury makes intelligent and gifted people, friendly, upright, articulate and lovable. They value art, beauty, athletic achievements, and fun. Regarding love, some of the men prefer males to females. They believe in, and strive for, excellence in all things. Venus and Mercury unfavorably aspected leads a person to shame himself by passing malicious gossip, stirring up trouble, and playing the rogue or villain. He or she can look fabulous while having the worst sort of intentions.

Aspects of Mercury

When Mercury alone and in good aspect governs the character, we have successful scholars, mathematicians, priests, and inventors, generous yet always with an eye on their own interests. They like to investigate and speculate about life's mysteries. Mercury alone in bad aspect makes crooks and schemers who are greedy yet can't think straight. These people are indecisive and the facts are always slipping their minds, so when they do make a choice they might not realize they have chosen the side of evil.

The Moon and Sun

The Moon influences all I have just said about the planets. If the Moon is rising and waxing, it enhances and secures the person's good qualities. If the Moon squares the north and south node [*Ptolemy does not explain the nodes*], the person is more adaptable and versatile. If the Moon is in conjunction with either node, this is a person bold and proactive. When the person is born as the Moon is waning or eclipsed, he or she is not so keen or energetic, and might hesitate to take the initiative.

The Sun also influences the planets. In favorable aspect, successes, honors, and humility are more likely. If the aspect is unfavorable, life is much harsher, work is a burden, and success is less likely.

3.15. Of Diseases of the Soul

We could say "diseases of the soul" begin in a person's character, when certain traits are taken to pathological extremes. People can sometimes choose to avoid these extremes, and other times they cannot help it.

We look again at the positions of the Moon and Mercury and the aspects between them and the angles. If there are no such aspects, check the natal chart for any planets that look like threats, either by opposing the Moon and/or Mercury, or by outnumbering the favorable planets. This situation causes diseases of the soul. Those include seizures, insanity, perversions and addictions, piled on to any negative traits and tendencies described in the previous chapter.

When the Moon and Mercury are unrelated by any aspect and additionally have no aspects to the ascendant, Saturn or Mars can overcome the chart by opposing or surrounding the Moon and Mercury. If you see Saturn by day and Mars by night, these conditions trigger seizures. Saturn by night and Mars by day cause violent insanity, especially if the zodiac signs Cancer, Virgo, or Pisces are involved. Saturn in conjunction with the new Moon, or Mars in conjunction with the full Moon, are also negative influences, especially if the signs Sagittarius or Pisces are involved.

When Saturn and Mars overcome the chart but do not aspect the ascendant or each other, the disease can remain latent and hidden, even though it is chronic. When those planets are in the western half of the chart and Jupiter and Venus are on or near the ascendant, chances for a cure increase. Jupiter's cure is doctors, diet, or drugs. Venus's cure is prayer and the help of the gods.

But if you reverse those conditions and have Jupiter and Venus setting, and Saturn and Mars rising, the disease is incurable and sufferers become notorious for their frequent seizures or bouts of dangerous insanity. Demonic possession causes agonizing thoughts and terrifying hallucinations, the chances increasing if Saturn and Mars are rising and favorable planets are setting. The Sun and Mars rising in opposition to the favorable planets incites insanity; Jupiter and Mercury cause epilepsy; and Venus rising opposite the favorable planets causes episodes of "possession."

The above are things that sufferers cannot control. Next we discuss the compulsions people can control but refuse to. Particularly noticeable are the sexual compulsions afflicting men and women.

Above we discussed the illnesses rooted in the positions of the Moon and Mercury. We can find sexual aberrations by looking now at the Moon and Sun and how they aspect the planets Mars and Venus. We interpret these aspects differently for men than for women.

When the Sun and Moon are in masculine signs and unattended by Mars or Venus, the men have normal sex drives but the women have sex drives like men's and are promiscuous. If Mars or Venus, or both, are furthermore in masculine signs or made masculine by position, the men are such sex fiends that if adult females are not around they take whatever they can get, any way they can get it. Under these aspects, women lust for and eyeball other women. If Venus alone is masculine, their sexual behavior stays secret. If Mars alone is masculine, the women don't hide it and openly call their female lovers their "wives."

When in a chart the Sun and Moon are in feminine signs and Mars and Venus are nowhere nearby, the females love sex with men, but the males will want men, and openly. If Venus happens also to be in a feminine sign, the women will do anything with any man, and the men take on the feminine role in sex acts, although these activities stay secret. But if Mars is feminized also, both the men and women are practically public property, and everybody talks about how shocking and awful that is.

It matters in this case whether Mars and Venus are rising, because rising intensifies the masculine traits in either gender, and if they are setting, the feminine traits intensify. Saturn's involvement will contribute disease and disgrace; Jupiter will contribute more discretion and modesty; and Mercury contributes notoriety and emotional insecurity, but also grants the person versatility, and insight into where his or her life is leading.

Tetrabiblos

Book Four

4.1. What Life Will Bring
4.2. About Riches
4.3. Will Life Be Happy?
4.4. Which Occupation?
4.5. About Marriage and Love
4.6. Having Children
4.7. About Friends and Enemies
4.8. Travel Abroad
4.9. The Quality of Death
4.10. About the Ages of Man
4.11. Predictions Using Primary Directions

4.1. What Life Will Bring

Book Three was about reading a natal chart to find the general traits a person is conceived or born with. In Book Four we will discuss how a natal chart tells us about future conditions and events specific to an individual's life.

4.2. About Riches

Money and fame are the first particulars clients tend to ask about. The key to the answer is the natal chart's Part of Fortune. In Book Three when discussing longevity, we described what the Part of Fortune is and how to calculate it. But let me repeat:

To figure the individual's Part of Fortune, in my opinion it does not matter whether the birth occurred during daylight or at night.

The figuring is done in two steps:

1. Measure the number of degrees (maximum, 360 degrees) from the Sun to the Moon, following the zodiac in its normal order.

2. Measure this same number of degrees from the ascendant, following the zodiac in its normal order, and that leads you to the Part of Fortune point.

Like a planet, the Part of Fortune will be in one of the zodiac signs and one of the chart's houses, and can be interpreted accordingly. Unlike a planet, it has no traits beyond being an indicator of good fortune.

The Part of Fortune is always in a zodiac sign, so first we determine the planetary lord of that sign. We look for how favorably or unfavorably that planet is situated in the client's natal chart, and whether it makes favorable aspects to the other planets. If so, the person is rich, especially if the Sun and Moon make favorable aspects to the planetary lord. Saturn as the lord generates riches through construction, farming, or shipping. Jupiter brings money through inheritance, trusts, or priesthood. With Mars, military service and high rank in any profession bring money. Venus means money comes through gifts from women or friends. Mercury brings money through trade or through public speaking: acting or lecturing, for example.

In a special way, a wealth-giving Saturn also brings inheritances if Jupiter makes a favorable aspect to it, or if Jupiter is at the ascendant or the midheaven, or in a bicorporeal sign: Gemini, Virgo, Sagittarius, or Pisces.

A rich client might lose his or her money if the less favorable planets somehow outweigh the favorable ones. The ruling planets should be of the same sect (daytime or nighttime) for financial security.

We can predict approximately when an inheritance will come by looking at Jupiter and Saturn as they transit the natal chart and approach the angles and the houses numbered 2, 5, 8, and 11.

4.3. Will Life Be Happy?

The Sun and Moon's positions, and those of the planets nearby, give people what they need to be happy: dignity and the esteem of others.

A client's children will become eminent or powerful if all of these conditions are met:

- both Sun and Moon are in masculine signs
- either one or both the luminaries is on an angle
- the subject was born in the daytime and all the other five planets "attend" the Sun
- the subject was born at night and all the other five planets "attend" the Moon

If the attending planets are on angles or in aspect to the midheaven, the children can actually rise to rule the world. That's even truer when the attending planets are to the right of the midheaven or ascendant: in the last five degrees of House 12, or in House 10.

If all this is true except that the Sun is in a masculine sign while the Moon is in a feminine sign, the children will become generals, judges, priests, or others with power over life and death.

If the Sun and Moon are angular in masculine signs but the five planets are not attending on or aspecting them, the children will have prominent roles and status in the temples, in the royal court, in civil service, or the military.

If the Sun and Moon are not angular, although most of the attending planets are either angular or in aspect to the angles, the children advance in their occupations but overall have moderate success.

If the Sun and Moon are not angular and the attending planets aren't angular either, the children will be ordinary and undistinguished. If it happens that the Sun and Moon are not angular and also on top of that they are both in feminine signs and not attended by the favorable planets, children will live humbly or even wretchedly.

For further details about the subject's future, the astrologer must examine more closely the relationships between all the planets and exactly how they "attend" the Sun or Moon. With favorable planets "attending," predict independence and security. With Saturn and Mars "attending," any prominence or fame is relatively brief or unstable. If Saturn is the most prominent planet "attending," expect material wealth, and with more wealth comes greater power. If Jupiter or Venus stands out among the "attending" planets, money and power come through gifts, prizes, or charity. Power through Mars comes through military rank, heroism, or the ability to intimidate others. Power through Mercury comes via intellectual efforts, education, planning, and goal setting.

4.4. Which Occupation?

There are two ways to determine the planetary lord of a person's occupation or career: from the Sun and from the chart's culminating sign.

Try the Sun method first. Look for the planet that rises closest to the morning Sun and then the planet nearest the midheaven, especially if it's favorably linked to the Moon. If those planets are one and the same, that is the only planet necessary to our reading.

If there is one planet rising closest, by degree, to the morning Sun and a different one at the midheaven and linked to the Moon, both planets govern the person's occupation, yet one planet is probably more influential than the other. Use what you have learned to decide which planet matters a little more.

If there's no planet rising close to the Sun or at the midheaven, use the planetary lord of the midheaven. People with this type of chart tend not to be gainfully employed but have duties or pastimes instead. Those can also be called "occupations."

After you single out the planet that governs the occupation, the subject's Mars, Venus, and Mercury in their zodiac signs provide more detailed information. But first, the planetary lords and the occupations they govern:

Mercury: Mercury governs the professions that depend on documents: writers, businesspeople, teachers, retailers and wholesalers, financiers, astrologers and advisers, temple administrators, and so on. If Saturn is favorably linked to Mercury, these people become landlords, proprietors, dream interpreters, or people who pursue their faith in order to feel inspired or connect with prophecy. Jupiter linked to that Mercury creates lawyers, orators, and scholars who will associate with eminent people.

Venus: Venus governs the professions that provide luxuries, such as winemakers, hoteliers, fashion and salon workers and beauty consultants, and artisans such as painters. If Saturn is favorably linked to Venus, the client will deal in luxury items such as jewelry or perfume, or practice unsavory arts such as sorcery and pimping. Jupiter favorably linked to Venus brings athletic or other types of honors, and men whose occupations or success depend on women.

Mars: When Mars aspects the Sun, the occupations are often related to fire, such as cooks and chefs, smiths, brickmakers, and miners. Mars without an aspect to the Sun creates people who work with iron, lumber, or stone: foundry workers, masons, quarry workers, jewelers, lumberjacks, shipbuilders, and those who work under them. Mars in aspect to Saturn signifies occupations having to do with water or liquids: sailors, animal keepers, plumbers, and morticians, for example. Mars in aspect to Jupiter creates soldiers, servants, tavern keepers, ferrymen, and temple acolytes.

If the person's occupation happens to have two planetary lords:

If they are Mercury and Venus, the client's occupation will be in the arts, and that is especially true if those planets are in mutual reception. Some possible occupations could be acting, poetry, music, weaving, singing, sculpting, or dancing—and also, dealing in slaves. If Saturn is in aspect with Mercury and Venus, the same is true except we add clothiers to that list of possible occupations. If Jupiter is in aspect, we have lawyers, accountants, teachers, and politicians.

If the two planetary lords are Mercury and Mars, the clients' occupations could be: builder, sculptor, physician and surgeon, wrestler, and also an adulterer, complainer, forger, and troublemaker. If Saturn is in aspect to Mercury and Mars, expect villains, murderers, cattle thieves, and burglars. If Jupiter aspects these two planets, these people occupy themselves as clever professional gossips and commentators. They are energetic, argumentative, and quick to make enemies and brandish weapons.

If Venus and Mars together govern the career, employment might include farming, metalworking including precious metals, pharmacy, perfumery, and membership in military-style drill or marching teams. Saturn aspecting these planets creates gravediggers, funeral directors, professional mourners, sacred-animal caretakers, and people attracted to occult mysteries and rites, especially those involving blood or mourning. Jupiter aspecting these planets creates matchmakers, chaperones, mediums and oracles, temple-dwellers, and sacred-instrument bearers. They can live on their earnings but are irresponsible and selfish.

Now that we know the planet or planets ruling the client's possible occupation, we focus on the zodiac signs they're in. The zodiac signs contribute yet another factor as we try to pinpoint the person's occupation.

Gemini, Virgo, Sagittarius, and Aquarius, signs with human beings as their symbols, encourage scientific occupations or service to humanity.

Signs with four-legged-animal symbols, such as Leo and Sagittarius, encourage occupations in practical professions such as sales, engineering, construction, and carpentry.

The signs of the equinoxes and solstices, Aries, Cancer, Leo, and Capricorn, encourage occupations in agriculture, religion, surveying, bartering, weights and measures, or interpreting.

The "terrestrial" signs, Aries, Taurus, Scorpio and Sagittarius, and the "aquatic" sign Pisces encourage water-related or plant-related occupations, or work that preserves, such as mortuary work or pickling.

If the Moon is the lord of the career and is together with Mercury separating from any conjunctions, and is in the signs Taurus, Cancer, and Capricorn, it creates diviners and clairvoyants, ritualists, and those who read omens in bottled liquids. In Sagittarius and Pisces we have conjurers and callers of spirits, in Virgo and Scorpio magicians, astrologers, psychics, and seers. In Leo we have dream interpreters, exorcists, and channelers.

All these things combined will point us toward a conclusion about the person's occupation. The planetary lords let us know the quality of their work and occupational experience. When the planetary lord or lords are rising or angular, they make bosses and chiefs; when setting or apart from the angles, they make subordinates. When favorable planets overwhelm the configuration, work is profitable, reputable, and showered with praise. Overwhelm the configuration with unfavorable planets and the work is shoddy and done resentfully. Saturn opposing the configuration brings on-the-job injuries, Mars in opposition brings nerve and notoriety, and Saturn and Mars together opposing the configuration indicates total career failure.

We can time the good and bad periods in a career by calculating when the planets involved will be in aspect to the chart's ascendant or descendant.

4.5. About Marriage and Love

The Moon's position in a male's natal chart predicts the type of marriage he will have. The Moon in the eastern quadrants means the man marries young or marries a woman his own age. The Moon in the western quadrants means a late marriage or marriage to an older woman.

If the Moon in a man's chart is 15 degrees or fewer from the Sun yet in aspect with Saturn, he stays a bachelor. Expect only one marriage if the Moon is placed in a zodiac sign represented by a single figure, and multiple marriages if the Moon is in Gemini, Virgo, Sagittarius, or Pisces, or if the Moon makes multiple aspects to planets in those signs. The Moon aspecting Saturn means he gets a hard-working, humorless wife. Aspecting Jupiter it brings a self-respecting wife who is an expert household manager. Aspecting Mars, expect a boisterous wife, and aspecting Venus, expect a pretty and charming wife. With the Moon aspecting Mercury, expect a brainy and perceptive wife. If Venus is well aspected with Jupiter, Saturn, or Mercury, the wife is demonstrative with her husband and children, and frugal. If Venus is aspected by Mars, the wife is irritable and emotionally cold.

In a woman's chart, the Sun hints at the type of man she will marry, and approximately when. Count as the Sun's eastern quadrants the three zodiac signs preceding the rising sign and the three preceding the setting sign. If the Sun is in one of those quadrants, the woman marries young or marries a younger man; if not, she marries late or to an older man. Expect one marriage if the Sun is in a zodiac sign represented by a single figure, or if the Sun is aspected by a planet in the chart's eastern quadrants. Expect multiple marriages if the Sun is in Gemini, Virgo, Sagittarius, or Pisces and the Sun makes multiple aspects to planets in the chart's eastern quadrants.

The Sun in aspect to Saturn signifies a sedate and industrious husband. The Sun in aspect to Jupiter brings a generous, dignified husband. Aspecting Mars, the husband is emotionally unavailable, restless, and a self-styled rebel. Aspecting Venus, the husband is handsome and fastidious. Aspecting Mercury, expect a frugal and practical husband. If Venus makes an aspect to Saturn, the husband's energy and sex drive are below normal. If Venus makes an aspect to Mars, he is passionate, demanding, and apt to cheat. Venus in aspect to Mercury means he finds boys enchanting.

Marriages are most durable when the couple's Sun signs and Moon signs are in trine or sextile aspect with each other. This is especially true if his Sun is in her Moon sign and her Moon is in his Sun sign. That's even truer if the husband's Moon favorably aspects his wife's Sun. Marriages can be fragile and the spouses become enemies if their Suns and Moons are in disjunct signs, or are in opposition or square aspect to each other.

A marriage is most agreeable and secure when favorable planets aspect harmonious Suns and Moons. A marriage is disagreeable, unprofitable, or unstable when unfavorable planets aspect otherwise harmonious Suns and Moons.

If the Suns and Moons are not harmonious but favorable planets still support them, the marriage survives rough patches and the spouses reconcile. Abusive and violent marriages are those with inharmonious Suns and Moons bolstered by unfavorable planets, and they end in divorce. If Mercury alone aspects inharmonious Suns and Moons, the couple is quarrelsome and everyone knows it. When Venus and Mercury together aspect inharmonious Suns and Moons, the husband and wife are adulterous, or are tempted to poison or otherwise harm each other.

If Venus, Mars, and Saturn are in favorable aspect to the Sun and Moon, the marriage is a recognized, legal marriage. Venus in favorable aspect to Mars shows marriage between people of similar age, because Venus is exalted in Taurus and Mars in Capricorn, and those two zodiac signs are in trine aspect to each other. Venus in favorable aspect with Saturn shows marriage between a young and an older person.

Venus in a favorable aspect to Mars creates sexual attraction, but if Mercury is involved, there's more than a whiff of scandal. If Mercury is in Capricorn or Pisces, marriage to a relative is possible. If in a man's chart Venus is with the Moon, he might marry a woman and then her sister or another female relative. In a woman's chart, Jupiter with the Moon means a woman will marry her own relatives or marry a man and then his brother.

Venus and Saturn sharing a favorable aspect create solid marriages, and if Mercury is involved, the marriage benefits both parties. Add the influence of Mars to this, and marriage will instead bring out the worst in the couple. Venus in aspect to both Saturn and Mercury brings marriages between people of a similar age, but if Venus is farther to the east than both Saturn and Mercury, the spouse will be younger, and if farther to the west, the spouse will be older.

If you see Venus in its home sign, Libra, plus Saturn in its home sign, Capricorn (and remember that Saturn is exalted in Libra), the spouse will be a relative. If, in addition to that, the Moon is at the ascendant or the midheaven, men will marry their mothers, aunts, or stepmothers, and women will marry their sons, nephews, or stepfathers. The Sun at the ascendant or midheaven will make the men marry their daughters or their own daughters-in-law; and the women will marry their fathers, uncles, or stepfathers.

It's best if the planets for marriages are all in feminine signs or masculine signs. If the planets are in signs of mixed gender and also in the top right or lower right quadrant, the relationship is immoral. If the planets are on or near the star clusters in the face and hind parts of the constellation Aries, in the face of Taurus, in the jar of Aquarius, or the face of Capricorn, the marriage is made for reasons considered sick or obscene. Add to this Venus and Saturn sitting at the ascendant and midheaven, and the couple flaunts their behavior. If Venus and Saturn are at the descendant and nadir, the couple's children are born with genital abnormalities or, if Mars is involved, the males have no genitalia or lose them, and both genders are sterile or sexually nonfunctional.

About Love and Attraction

In a man's chart, Mars reveals how a man in love will behave. When his Mars is aspected by Jupiter but unconnected with Venus or Saturn, when in love he acts honorably and naturally. Mars in aspect to Saturn means he is too wary, cold, or asexual to fall in love. Mars aspected by both Venus and Jupiter makes a passionate man able to restrain himself when necessary. Mars aspected by Venus alone, or by Venus plus Jupiter with no involvement whatsoever of Saturn, the planet of restraint, indicates a man who beds every woman available, and if one of those planets is an evening star and another a morning star, either gender will do. If both are evening stars, he lusts for females only. When in this configuration Venus and Jupiter happen to be in feminine signs, he lusts for men; in masculine signs, he wants males of any age. If both Venus and Jupiter are morning stars, he loves boys.

If in this configuration Venus is farther to the west than Mars, the man prefers female servants, slaves, and foreigners. If Mars is to the west of Venus, he wants married or high-status females only.

In a woman's natal chart, Venus shows how she behaves when she's in love. In favorable aspect with Mercury or Jupiter, the woman is pure and mild-mannered. If Saturn is not at all associated with the woman's Venus, she is passionate, but cautious about when and how she expresses passion. When Mars is the only planet in aspect to a woman's Venus, she is wanton and careless. Jupiter present in this configuration, along with Mars within the Sun's rays [*so near the Sun that its glow makes Mars invisible*], might give her a preference for lower-class men, slaves, and foreigners. If Venus is with them and above the horizon, the woman wants only high-status men or aims to become her master's or boss's mistress, even if she is already married.

If Venus, Mars, and Jupiter are all rendered feminine because of their placements in the chart, the woman is sexually passive, but if they're all rendered masculine she desires other women. Saturn's influence on this configuration, if Saturn by position is rendered feminine, will by itself create a loose woman. If Saturn is rising and in a masculine position, people call her immoral but she calls herself a sexual rebel. Jupiter acting on this combination makes a woman more discreet. Mercury there instead makes the woman careless and notorious.

4.6. Having Children

After asking about marriage, the client's next question is usually about children. That answer will be in the chart's midheaven, or in aspect to the midheaven, or in the chart's House 11. If the chart has no planets in those places, look at the planets at the nadir and in House 5.

The Moon, Jupiter, or Venus in those places means several children, and if Mercury aspects those planets and is a morning star, Mercury reinforces that conclusion. Saturn and Mars in those places indicate few children or none, and Mercury in aspect to those planets, when Mercury is an evening star, confirms that the children will be few.

The Moon, Jupiter, and Venus grant children. If one of those planets happens to be alone at the chart's midheaven, or in aspect to the midheaven, or in House 11, expect one child. If the lone planet is in Virgo or Pisces (the two signs which are both bicorporeal and feminine), or in fertile signs such as Cancer, Scorpio, and Pisces, predict two children or more. Masculine planets aspecting the Sun give male children, and feminine planets aspecting the Sun give female children.

If the Moon, Jupiter, and Venus are poorly aspected, or in sterile places in the chart such as Leo or Virgo, the children are disappointing or will not stay with the parent for long. If the Sun, Mars, and Saturn occupy Leo or Virgo, and the favorable planets do not mitigate their influence, the person will be childless. The Sun, Mars, and Saturn combination, when it's in feminine zodiac signs or in the signs Cancer, Scorpio, and Pisces, even when the favorable planets make favorable aspects, may grant children who might not live long.

When both favorable and unfavorable planets happen to be in aspect with the fertile signs, Cancer, Scorpio and Pisces, some or all of the children might be lost. Whether all or only a few are lost depends on whether favorable or unfavorable planets dominate the chart. Figure this by counting how many planets aspect the fertile signs of Cancer, Scorpio, and Pisces. A larger number of favorable or powerful planets, in either sect, or at the angles, or occupying houses 2, 5, 8, or 11, indicate that losses will be fewer.

The children will become famous for their accomplishments if the planet ruling Cancer (the Moon) and the planet ruling Pisces (Jupiter) are rising and placed in the houses they rule. If those same planets are setting and in places belonging to the opposite sect, and their houses are ruled by the unfavorable planets, the children will be average or less.

Step back now, and look at the whole natal chart. If the Moon and Jupiter harmonize with the whole chart and also with the Part of Fortune, the children will be beautiful and receive a substantial parental inheritance. The Moon and Jupiter and the Part of Fortune in opposing or disjunct positions indicate fractious, troublemaking children who receive no inheritance.

The Moon, Jupiter, and Venus in favorable aspect to each other means the children will like and respect each other. If those planets are disjunct or in opposition to each other, it means the siblings fight. For a client who wants to know more about children, create a second chart, using as its ascendant point the position of the natal planet best suited to granting children to this particular client.

4.7. About Friends and Enemies

When inquiring about a person's friends and enemies, and the intensity of either type of relationship, it's best to have at hand the natal charts of both people involved and compare in them these four important friendship points: the degrees of the Sun, Moon, ascendant, and Part of Fortune.

If the two people have one or more of these same points in the same zodiac sign, or if one or all of those points are in mutual reception, and particularly if the ascendants are about 17 degrees apart, predict a strong and lasting friendship. Those points in disjunct or opposing signs indicate active antagonism. If there are no such contacts, then if those points happen to be in signs that harmonize, or are in trine or sextile aspect, the friendship is more casual. If those points are in square aspect, any enmity is mild.

Transiting Mars and Saturn through these configurations signify periods of estrangement or talking behind each other's backs. Favorable planets entering and transiting through these configurations can cause former friends to reconcile.

Both friends and enemies are acquired in three ways: by preference; by necessity; or made through pleasure or pain. If the crucial points in their natal charts are harmonious, the friendship blends all three elements. Between enemies, those three elements do not blend but instead stand out separately.

If, of the four important friendship indicators, the pair's Suns and Moons harmonize, then it's a friendship by choice: the best kind. When they don't harmonize, it's the worst type of enmity. When the Parts of Fortune harmonize, the friendship grew from necessity. When the ascendants harmonize, the pair is linked through either pleasure or pain.

If their ascendants are in the same zodiac sign or one of their ascendants happens to be in the next sign but close by, the person with the ascendant rising first directs the friendship or the antagonism. For example, a person whose ascendant is 16 degrees of Scorpio directs the relationship she has with a person whose ascendant is 27 degrees of Scorpio. If, between the four important friendship points, one of the pair has more trines and sextiles, that person benefits most from the friendship or the enmity.

If the question is about when the client might make temporary or occasional friends or enemies, we calculate how much time it will take for a certain planet on Person A's natal chart to "trade places" with a certain planet on Person B's natal chart. [*Because Ptolemy's method depends on the locale and season, the result of the following will be an approximation only.*]

With this method, each person involved takes a turn being Person A and Person B. Measure in each chart, following the zodiac, the number of degrees between the said planets for each. Then add those numerals and divide by 15. Each degree can equal either one day or one year.

A's Saturn trading with B's Jupiter: Friendship will be made through introductions, farming, or inheritance.

A's Saturn trading with B's Mars: Enemies made through premeditated arguments and schemes.

A's Saturn trading with B's Venus: Friendships made through relatives, but these friendships are soon over.

A's Saturn trading with B's Mercury: A friendship or marriage of convenience, or an alliance for ritual spiritual purposes.

A's Jupiter trading with B's Mars: Friendships through property ownership or both being rich or otherwise high-status people.

A's Jupiter trading with B's Venus: Friendships through women or faith-based associations.

A's Jupiter trading with B's Mercury: Friendship through a meeting of minds.

A's Mars trading with B's Venus: Romantic, adulterous, or illegitimate relationships, all very brief.

A's Mars trading with B's Mercury: Loud arguments, open enmities, and lawsuits rooted in business issues or poisonings.

A's Venus trading with B's Mercury: Friendships through the arts, or made by correspondence or through women.

How intense or beneficial will these temporary relationships be? To answer that, we look at the relationships between the above planets and the four friendship points: the degrees of the Sun, Moon, ascendant, and Part of Fortune. If any of those is on one of the four angles, or on the other's Part of Fortune, or in the houses where the Sun and Moon reside, the relationship should be intense. The farther those bodies are from the friendship points, the more forgettable the friendship. If there are more contacts with unfavorable planets, the relationship is bad for both. More contacts with favorable planets indicate that both parties will benefit.

Relationships between master and slave are governed by a natal chart's House 12, "House of the Evil Spirit." Look for the planets that naturally govern that house, and also for planets in that house or in opposition to it. It is best for that particular relationship if those planets harmonize or have similar natures.

4.8. Travel Abroad

The Moon in particular is important when a client asks about travel. Predict travel if the Sun and Moon, but especially the Moon, are at the angles. If the Moon is declining or setting, the client will travel abroad, or move and settle in another country. Mars declining or setting sometimes indicates the same if it is in square aspect or in opposition to either the Sun or Moon.

The Part of Fortune in the zodiac signs which indicate travel [*Ptolemy does not say which signs those are*] means the person spends his or her entire life abroad. Favorable planets aspecting the Sun, Moon, and Part of Fortune, when those indicate travel, mean that the travel experience will be honorably profitable and the traveler returns with no delays. Aspects from unfavorable planets mean the journey will deplete rather than enrich the traveler, and maybe even injure him or her, and the return trip can be dangerous.

Remember, when a client asks about future travel, to consider also the planets ruling the locales the traveler will start from and hopes to visit, and the aspects those planets make to the chart.

We can predict, in a general way, where travelers might be going:

- if the Sun and Moon are in the chart's left lower quadrant: east or south.
- if Sun and Moon are in the western quadrants: north or west.

- If the zodiac signs causing travel are those of a single figure (not bicorporeal), journeys will be few and far between.

- If the signs indicating travel are Gemini, Virgo, Libra, Sagittarius or Pisces, travel is frequent and for extended periods.

- When Jupiter and Venus govern the destination as well as the Sun and Moon, it will be a safe, pleasant journey, its expenses often paid by government authorities or the traveler's friends. Mercury appearing in this mix means the trip will be profitable either materially or socially.

- When Saturn and Mars govern the destination, and especially when they oppose each other, the trip is dangerous, with a risk of shipwreck if those planets are in watery zodiac signs.

- If Saturn and Mars control the luminaries, and especially if they oppose each other, predict rough going through desert places.

- If Saturn and Mars are in the solid signs of Taurus, Leo, Scorpio and Aquarius, there is danger of falling, or trouble from high winds.

- If Saturn and Mars are in the solstitial or equinoctial signs (Aries, Cancer, Libra, Capricorn), provisions run low and travelers risk their health.

- If Saturn and Mars are in zodiac signs which have human form, danger might come through robbers or pirates. In the terrestrial signs, threats come from animals or earthquakes. If Mercury happens to be there also, the traveler might be confronted with hotheaded accusations or animals that bite or sting.

For details about the traveler's career, property, body, or dignity, see the houses that each govern these matters, find their planetary lords, and decide from there. Look also at the planets, excluding the Sun and Moon, about to enter the zodiac signs that cause travel.

4.9. The Quality of Death

Determine the planetary lord of a person's death by referring to the planetary lord you found when preparing to calculate the length of life [*See Book Three, chapters 10 and 11*]. That planet is most lethal when on the descendant, but death might also occur when that planet, in other places in the chart, is affected by "rays." "Rays" [*most likely from Saturn and Mars*] can influence the degrees ahead of and behind them, creating danger zones in the chart. Take note of the zodiac signs and houses these danger zones are in, and of any planets approaching those danger zones.

The effects of the planets when they act as the chart's lord of death:

Saturn: Long or chronic illnesses, chills and fever, exposure to cold, water retention, diseases of joints and connective tissue.

Jupiter: Pneumonia, strangulation, stroke, spasms, headaches, heart conditions, digestive disorders.

Mars: Fevers, especially those that spike and recede; sudden strokes, kidney problems, hemorrhages, miscarriages or childbirth, plagues, coughing up blood, and heat stroke.

Venus: Digestive and liver problems, cancers, fistulas, poisoning.

Mercury: Insanity, carelessness, depression, epilepsy, coughing up and spitting phlegm, dehydration.

People die natural deaths when 1) their lords of death occupy compatible places and 2) no other destructive planet overwhelms them. People die violent and conspicuous deaths when Saturn and Mars are in conjunction, opposition, or square aspect to the danger zones, or if those two planets afflict the Sun, the Moon, or both. For more detail, see what zodiac signs those planets are in, and the aspects the signs and the other planets make to them.

Saturn, when it's a nighttime planet and it squares or opposes the Sun and is in a solid zodiac sign, brings death by suffocation, including being trampled or hanged. The same is true when Saturn is setting and the Moon is approaching it. Saturn in a sign symbolized by an animal brings death by wild animals, and if an afflicted Jupiter is in unfavorable aspect to that Saturn, that death might happen publicly or while fighting animals for sport. A rising Saturn opposite the Sun or Moon could mean death in prison. Saturn in aspect to Mercury causes deaths by venomous bites, and if Venus is present, poisonings or murder arranged by women. Saturn in Virgo or Pisces, aspected by the Moon, might mean drowning. If Saturn and the Sun are both at the chart's midheaven or nadir, death might result from a fall.

Mars squaring or opposing the Sun or Moon from a sign of the other sect and in a sign symbolized by a human form, brings death from enemy attacks and suicide. If Venus is in unfavorable aspect to the Sun, Moon, and Mars, women are murdered or they are murderers.

Mercury in unfavorable aspect to the Sun or Moon signifies death by robbers, pirates, or other criminals. If in the "mutilated" or "imperfect" zodiac signs of Taurus, Cancer, Scorpio, or Sagittarius, or in the Gorgon head that holds the malefic star Caput Algol, death comes by decapitation and mutilation; in Scorpio and Taurus, death by convulsions or surgeons who cut, amputate, or cauterize. In this configuration, Mercury at the midheaven or the nadir signifies crucifixion. Opposite the ascendant, Mercury causes death by burning. In the signs representing quadrupeds, the person might be crushed to death; for example, beneath a collapsing building. If Jupiter is afflicted, the person is condemned to death by commanders or other authorities.

Saturn and Mars together opposing the Sun, Moon, ascendant, or midheaven, affect the circumstances of death for the worse. The planet occupying the danger zone foretells the type of death. Having both Saturn and Mars in a danger zone doubles its horror. The person's body might lie unburied and be eaten by animals if no favorable planets make aspects to the danger zones or to the nadir. Deaths abroad might result if Saturn or Mars occupies a danger zone that happens to be in House 3, 6, 9, or 12. That is especially true if the Moon is in opposition to or squares the danger zone.

4.10. About the Ages of Man

Never assume that what you deduce from a person's natal chart will come true unless you have factored in the general conditions that are truly basic and provide context: the person's country, culture, climate, and stage of life. By ignoring those factors you might predict that an Ethiopian will be born white, or advise an Egyptian, whose people marry their own kin, to marry an Italian when clearly it would be better if he married another Egyptian.

Take care that you are not predicting, for a baby, his wedding next year, or predicting new offspring for aged people.

The Seven Planets Governing the Ages of Man

There are seven ages of man, matching the spheres and qualities of the seven planets. Astrologers, tailor your predictions and advice accordingly.

The Moon governs birth through age 3. Infants and toddlers, like the Moon, are supple and moist, consume liquid nourishment, and like the Moon change shape rather quickly.

Mercury governs ages 4 through 14: childhood. Children of this age begin to reason, speak well, and learn basics in school. Their individual personalities develop and flower.

Venus governs youth ages 15 through 22 who are developing sexually and find their impulses, good or bad, very hard to restrain.

The Sun is the lord of the middle sphere, and its influence lasts 19 years, from ages 23 through 41. During this time people master themselves and their actions, seek honors and status, and take life more seriously than before.

The next and fifth stage of life is governed by Mars and lasts 15 years, ages 42 through 56. People of this age begin thinking they have passed their prime without making their mark on the world, and might drive themselves even harder and develop worries and dwell on their aches and pains.

Jupiter, with its 12-year orbit, governs the subsequent 12 years, from ages 57 through 68. At that age a person doesn't care to do manual labor and might want to retire, but he or she knows there are still laurels and honors to win. People at this stage who do win honors are modest about it.

The seventh age of man is governed by Saturn. This period lasts from the end of the Jupiter age until death. Under Saturn, passions of the body and soul have cooled. Body and mind are well-worn, react more slowly, and meet with more challenges. People of this age can be depressed, easily offended, fussy, or sluggish.

That's the basic and very general information about the seven ages. Notice how the concept aligns with nature.

Beyond the Natal Chart

Besides the natal horoscope chart, you can cast a secondary, derivative horoscope for details about the client's particular concerns. The natal horoscope on its own will tell us about a person's body, soul, and journeys. Cast a horoscope with the person's Part of Fortune on the ascendant in order to learn more about his or her property and material holdings. The Moon used as the chart's ascendant tells us more about affection and marriage, and the Sun as the ascendant about personal achievement and honors. Use the midheaven as the ascendant to tease out details about the client's children, family, and friends, or his or her place in society or the community.

This is better than using the natal chart alone for all predictions. Perhaps it will shake loose the widespread belief that everything in a life, especially luck and happiness, is forever set in stone in the natal chart. A planet positioned low in the natal chart can be prominent in a Part of Fortune chart. This reflects the variety we meet with in life. Rarely are we perfectly happy or utterly devastated, because at any one time we are experiencing several life events and developments, some positive and some not. It's a blend. Humans aren't well adapted to living at one or the other extreme.

Bad things can indeed have good outcomes. A sad event such as a relative's death might lead to the good fortune of a fine inheritance. Negative and positive things co-exist and tend to balance each other out. For example, during a period of frustration and struggle on the job, one might also experience the joy of having a new son or daughter.

When interpreting any chart, do not concentrate on the unfavorable planets or unfavorable aspects and neglect the favorable ones. They all matter.

There are times in life when all seems blissful or when all seems lost. Setting up a chart for such a time might show all the favorable planets in a cluster, or, in the opposite case, all the unfavorable planets. Choose as the decisive planet in this chart the last planet in this cluster.

4.11. Predictions Using Primary Directions

To make predictions about events and their timing we use Primary Directions calculations as we did for figuring the length of life. This requires first a natal chart [*which must be accurate to the minute in order for the prediction's timing to be accurate*], then a chart aligned with diurnal motion.

Because the Earth turns once on its axis every 24 hours, providing us with the illusion that the stars drift continually westward, on any given day a chart's ascendant point, within the chart's ascending zodiac sign, rises one degree every four minutes, or 15 degrees per hour.

We want to find out and count how many degrees the ascendant must move until it makes any of the five major aspects to the natal chart's planets, angles, and fixed stars. The number of degrees is then translated into years. Five degrees? That means five years. That is how we time future events.

Notice that I said here "Any of the five major aspects," not solely the unfavorable ones.

It would be easier if the ecliptic were the same as the Earth's equator, but it is not. The ecliptic is offset at an angle of 23.5 degrees. So we must adjust our numbers to get the correct number of degrees. We then translate the degrees into units of time—most often, a year for each degree—to pinpoint the timing of future events by year, month, and day.

[*In the 21st century, astrological computer software is most often used to determine primary directions and their degrees of arc. For accurate predictions, birth times to the minute are still essential. A four-minute discrepancy between the recorded birth time and the actual birth time results in a prediction that is "off" by one year.*]

We will then figure out which planet rules a certain year of the person's life. Start with the sign that rules the ascendant. The planet ruling that sign is the "time lord" of the whole chart. From that planet count forward, sign by sign, the number of years from birth and see what sign you end up on. The planet that rules that sign is the "time lord" of that year.

Count forward from that sign the number of months since the birth. Each sign represents one month of 28 days [*some manuscripts say 30 days*]. The planetary ruler of the last sign you land on is the "time lord" of the months.

From there, count forward, sign by sign, the number of days since birth, with each sign equaling two and one-third days. After finishing that count, you will have the "time lord" of the days.

Should the "time lord" planets all be the same, expect (depending on the planet and its qualities) that the predicted event will be extremely favorable or extremely unfavorable.

A "time lord" planet aligned with its place in the natal chart, depending on the nature of that planet means the event will be either very good or very bad. Also look at the way each "time lord" planet aspects its original place in the natal chart. Favorable aspects affect the event positively; opposition aspects are unfavorable. The same goes for the Sun and Moon, except it's unfavorable if the Sun and Moon oppose or square their natal places.

Factors that go into predicting the event's timing:

- aspects between the zodiac signs that contain the time lords for the years and the months
- whether the time lords and their natures support each other or are antagonistic
- aspects between the zodiac signs the planets are currently transiting
- the relationship of the Sun and the Moon to the time lords of the years and the months.

Planets transiting or passing through the zodiac signs that hold the time lords can show the duration and impact of the predicted event. Saturn's transit is the most important because slow-moving Saturn is "lord of the general times" and rules the basis or foundation of your prediction. Jupiter's transit is important if you are looking at years. The transits of the Sun, Mars, Venus, and Mercury are important if you are looking at months, and the Moon if you are looking at days. Depending on their natures and the signs they are transiting, the planets' positions can intensify or obstruct the events predicted.

At times of great happiness or great unhappiness, the primary-direction chart as compared with the natal will often show the favorable planets in a cluster, or, in the case of unhappiness, the unfavorable ones. If the planets are not in a cluster, see where the planets in one chart make favorable or unfavorable aspects to each other. The higher the number of favorable aspects, the better.

That is how we predict the timing and quality of future events.

[*The most authoritative* Tetrabiblos *manuscripts break off here, without a conclusion. Over the centuries, concluding paragraphs have been added by others, including "Proclus." The conclusion that 1940 translator F.E. Robbins judged most authentic is used here:*]

The method I have presented harmonizes with nature.

Complete examples of predictive timing, including their results, are complicated and would be hard to explain here. As I wrote at the beginning, keep in mind that the powers of the planets in general situations apply in individual situations also. Astrologers, use good judgement when reading charts and making predictions for individuals.

Now that we've completed this survey of how to read natal charts, it is time to close this discussion.

INDEX

Angles, four, defined (see also Ascendant, Descendant, Midheaven, Nadir), *iii*, 15, 27
Anareta (see Lifespan)
Animals, in the zodiac, 39, 59, 68, 81, 88; livestock 4, 39, 41
Aquarius, 10, 13, 16-26, 34-36, 39-40, 44, 57, 62, 68-69, 71-72, 81, 83, 88
Aries, 10-11, 15-17, 20-27, 32-34, 36, 39-40, 43, 62, 68-71, 81, 83, 88
Ascendant, *iii-iv*, 15, 27-28, 39, 49-53, 55-59, 61-64, 66-69, 71, 75, 78-79, 82-83, 85-87, 89, 91-92
    calculating ascendant without a birth time, 51-52
    defined, 15, 50
    importance, 27-28, 50-52, 63
    in lifespan calculation, 61, 64-65
Aspects, planetary, defined, 18-19, 27; favorable and unfavorable, 18-19 (see also Conjunction; Opposition; Sextile; Square; Trine)
Astrologers, 3, 5-6, 28, 64, 66
    advice for, 3-8, 27-28, 31, 50-51, 60, 65, 70-72, 90-91
Astrological chart
    angles, four (also called "the four cardinal points"), 15 (see also Angles)
    birth (see Natal charts)
    dominant planet of, 33-34, 51-52, 64
    houses, astrological (see Twelve astrological houses)
    interpreting planetary aspects, 4, 27-28 (see Planetary aspects)
    quadrants, 10, 28, 55, 57-58, 71-72, 82-83, 87
    reading (see Reading Natal Charts)
    shape of, 18, 19, 24, 27
Astrology
    basics, 1-24, 27-28, 47-53
    Chaldean, 24-25
    and chance, 4, 5, 7
    defense of, 4-5
    Egyptian, 8, 24-25
    and free will, 8
    misconceptions about, 7-8, 50
    Ptolemy's outdated views about, *iii-iv*

uses of, 6-8
Bicorporeal zodiac signs, 16-17, 40, 57, 59, 71, 78, 85, 88
Birth chart (see Natal charts)
Birth horoscope (see Natal charts)
Birth time (see Natal charts)
Cancer, 10, 12, 16-17, 19-26, 34-36, 40, 43-44, 46, 57, 62, 68-71, 75, 81, 85, 88-89
Capricorn, 10, 13, 16-26, 33-34, 36, 40, 43-44, 62, 68-71, 81, 83, 88
Cardinal point, 15-16
Cardinal signs (see Zodiac signs)
Career or occupation, 53, 79-82, 88; planets and careers, 79, 81-82; zodiac signs and careers, 81
Character reading (see Reading natal charts)
Children (see Predictions about children)
Clouds, 46-47
Comets, 42; and weather, 46
Conjunction, planetary aspect, defined, 18-19
    approaching and separating, 27, 60, 67, 71, 81, 89
Conjunctions of:
    Sun, 45, 54, 56, 57, 60, 63, 68, 69; at midheaven 56, 59, 70, 89; at nadir, 56, 89
    Moon, 45, 56, 60, 63, 68-69, 71, 75; at midheaven 59, 70, 83; at nadir, 84
    Mercury, 7; at midheaven 89; at nadir, 89
    Venus, 56, 65; at midheaven 83; at nadir, 83-84
    Mars, 69, 75, 82, 89; at midheaven, 56, 70
    Jupiter, 83; at midheaven 78; at nadir, 84
    Saturn, 56, 57, 60, 75, 89; at midheaven, 56, 70, 83, 89; at nadir, 56, 83, 84, 89
Death (see Lifespan, and Quality of death)
Decans, defined, *iv*, 43; in weather forecasting, 43-44
Defense of astrology, 4-5
Degrees of orb, 27
Descendant, *iii*, 15-16, 27, 39-40, 53-59, 63, 65-66, 68-69, 75, 82-83, 88
Disjunct signs, 20, 28, 68, 72, 82, 85
Diurnal motion, 17, 32, 64, 91
Eclipses, solar and lunar, 37-42
    planetary rulers or 'lords' of, 40-42
    predictions from, 37-42

and zodiac signs, 39-40
Ecliptic, 22, 31, 36, 43, 33, 61, 65, 91
Egyptian, 8, 24-25, 43, 90
Equinoctial zodiac signs Aries and Libra, 16, 40, 43, 45, 88
Equinoxes, 15-17, 22, 26, 40, 43, 45, 81
Exalted and fallen planets, defined, 22-23; 40, 43, 45, 52-54, 62, 71-72, 81, 83; Table of, 23, 62
'Faces,' 26-27, 43, 56
Favorable and unfavorable aspects, defined, *iv*, 18-19
Favorable and unfavorable planets, defined, *iv*, 9, 91
    dual-natured planet Mercury, 9, 10, 11, 59, 65
    and eclipses, 40-42
Fixed stars, 11-15; in charts, 36-39, 40-41, 43, 45-46, 66-67, 91
    in constellations outside of the zodiac, 13-15
Four winds, 15-16
Gemini, 10, 12, 16-17, 19-26, 34-36, 40, 43-44, 57, 59, 62, 68, 70-71, 78, 81-82, 88
Health: disability, 68-70; mental, 70-72, 75-76; of parents, 55-57; physical, 68-69
Horoscope (see Natal charts)
Houses, astrological (see Twelve astrological houses)
Humours, theory of, 8-10
Jupiter, 4, 9-15, 20-27, 32-35, 37, 41-42, 56, 59, 62, 65, 67, 69-70, 72-73, 75-76, 78-90, 92
    natal Jupiter, 56, 65, 72, 75, 78, 84-86
Leo, 10, 12, 16-17, 19-21, 23-26, 32-34, 36, 40, 44, 57, 62, 68-69, 71-72, 81, 85, 88
Libra, 10, 12, 16-17, 21-26, 34-36, 40, 43-44, 62, 68, 70, 83, 88
Lifespan, 60-66
    accuracy of predictive formula, 64, 65
    Alcoccoden (ruling planet of the Hyleg), 63-66
    Anareta, defined 61; anaretic points 65; mitigation 65
    ascendant, 61
    calculation, 60-66
    calculation excludes accidents, crime, epidemics, natural disasters, war or self-harm, 7, 64
    confusion about, *iv*, 64
    defined, 61
    ethics of prediction, 64, 65

       exact birth time required, 65
       example of calculation, 66
       Hyleg, 61-66; ruling planet, 63
       planetary transits, 63, 65
Longevity (see Lifespan)
Looks and temperament, 66-68; zodiac signs and body types, 68
Love and attraction, 83-84
Luminaries, defined, 20
Lunar eclipses, (see Eclipses)
Marriage and love, 82-84, 91; compatible Sun-Moon aspects, 82-83; heterosexual, 82-83; homosexual, 74, 76, 82, 84; love and attraction, 53, 74, 82-84; planetary aspects, 82-84; sex drive, 73-74, 76, 84
Mars, 4, 9-15, 20-27, 32-35, 37, 41-42, 56, 58-60, 62-63, 65, 67-76, 78-90, 92
       natal Mars, 56, 58, 67-68, 72, 75, 78, 84-87
Mercury, 4, 9-15, 20-26, 33-36, 41-42, 59-60, 62, 65, 67, 69-76, 78-84, 86-90, 92
       natal Mercury, 67, 72, 75, 78, 82, 84, 86, 87
Meteors, 46
Midheaven,
       basics, 15-16, 27-28, 39
       in charts, 36-38, 40, 52-56, 58-59, 61-62, 64, 70, 72, 78-80, 83-85, 89, 91
Money and wealth, 53, 55, 60, 78
       calculating the Part of Fortune, 61-62, 78
       careers, 54, 79-82, 88
       inheritance, 56, 78, 85
       parents, 55-57, 85
       property, 74, 86, 91
Moon, 1, 3-5, 7-13, 16, 20-23, 25-27, 29, 31-32, 35-38, 40-43, 45-46, 50-51, 55-63, 67-72, 75-76, 78-92
       natal Moon, 36, 42, 51, 55-57, 67, 69, 71, 75, 78, 82-87
       and Sun (see Planets: Sun and Moon)
Moon phases, 4, 11, 32, 42-43, 45-46, 51, 56, 59, 63, 67, 69, 75; and weather, 42, 43, 45-46
Mutual reception, planets in, 71, 82, 86-87
Nadir, defined, *iii*, 10, 15, 16, 27, 39, 53, 55-56, 58, 71, 83-84, 89 (see also Conjunctions of)
Natal charts (also called birth charts or horoscopes),

    ascendant, calculating without a birth time, 51-52
    birth time, defined, 50
    examples of questions and answers, 54-55
    and free will, 8
    interpreting (see Reading natal charts)
    limitations of, 4, 5-8, 17, 50, 91
    moment of birth, 50-52
    personality readings (see Reading natal charts)
    planets (see Planets)
    predictions from (see Predictions)
    quadrants, 10, 55, 57-58, 71-72, 82-83, 87
    questions a natal chart can answer, 52-55
    ruling planets, 53-56, 58, 61
    usefulness, 6-8
    variations of, 57, 91

Nations, astrology of, 32-38; eclipses, 37; zodiac signs governing nations, 36
Natural disasters, 7, 61
Nodes, lunar *(Ptolemy does not explain)*, 75
Opposition, planetary aspect, defined, 18-19; 20, 54, 57
Oppositions to:
    Sun, 51, 56, 57, 60, 69-70, 75, 82, 87, 89, 92
    Moon, 51, 60, 69-70, 75, 83, 85, 87, 89, 92
    Mercury, 75, 89
    Venus, 76, 85
    Mars, 56, 60, 63, 75, 81, 87-89
    Jupiter, 85
    Saturn, 56, 60, 63, 81, 88, 89
    Ascendant, 57, 63, 89
    Descendant, 57, 68-69, 88
    Midheaven, 28-29, 89
Orbs (degrees between planets), defined, 27-28
Parallel, planetary, 27
Parents, predictions about, 55-57
Part of Fortune calculation, 61-62, 78; as Hyleg, 62; meaning, 61, 78, 86; natal, 56, 61, 78, 85-86
Personality (see Reading natal charts)

Pisces, 10, 13, 17-26, 34-36, 39-40, 44, 57, 59, 62, 68, 70-71, 75, 78, 81-83, 85, 88-89
Planetary aspects,
    defined, 18-19, 27 (see also Conjunction, Opposition, Sextile, Square, Trine)
Planets (see also individual planet names)
    above and below the horizon, 28, 57, 61-63, 71
    aspects (see Planetary aspects)
    'attending', defined, 55-56
    basics, 8-11
    culminating, 55
    dominating planet, identifying, 51-52, 72
        eclipse charts, 39-41
        effects on a natal chart, 72-75, 85
    nations, 33-35
    'daytime' and 'nighttime', 10-11
    'Eastern' or 'Western', 10, 71
    exalted and fallen, 22-23; Table of, 62
    favorable and unfavorable, 9
    governing body parts, 68-69
    governing the Seven Ages of Man, 90
    'leading' and 'following', 27, 44, 76
    'lords,' also called 'rulers', 20, 39, 78-81, 88
    'masculine' and 'feminine' planets, 10
    'masculine' and 'feminine' zodiac signs, 17-18
    at midheaven, 28, 89 (see also Conjunctions of)
    in mutual reception, 71, 82, 86-87
    at nadir, 56, 71, 83-84, 89
    natal (see the planet's name)
    shaping looks and temperament 66-68
    orbs of influence (see Orbs)
    powers and qualities, basic, 8-9
    'rays', 60, 84
    retrograde, 11, 27, 31, 55, 67, 71
    rising, or ascendant, 5, 10-11, 27-28, 31, 37-39, 45-46, 50-52, 54, 60, 66-69, 75-76, 80-82, 84-86, 89
    rulers of fixed stars, 11-15
    ruling planets, also called 'lords': of charts 20-21, 54-55, 72-75

    of eclipses, 40-42
    of zodiac signs, 21
  'sects', defined, 10
  setting, or descendant, 10, 27, 38, 45, 54-55, 67, 69, 71, 75-76, 81-82, 85, 87, 89
  stationing, defined, 11; 37-38, 54, 67, 71
  Sun and Moon, *iii*, 1, 4-5, 7-9, 20-21, 25, 31, 36-38, 41, 45-46, 50-51, 55-56, 59-60, 69-70, 75-76, 78-79, 83, 87-88, 92
  traits of each planet, 8-9
  weak, in natal charts, 22, 28, 55, 57
Predestination, 7
Predictions, 3-8, 27-28, 49-93 (see also: Predictions through natal charts; Reading natal charts)
  faulty or incomplete, 5, 8
  challenges of, 3, 5-8, 70
Predictions about children, 84-85
  charts for infants under one year old, 60, 61, 64
  children's traits and future prospects, 79, 85
  conception charts, 50-51, 58
  gender prediction, 85
  moment of birth, 50-52
  mortality, 60
  multiple births or congenital conditions, 52, 58-60, 69
  number of children, 84-85
  planets governing childhood, 90
  siblings, number of, 57
Predictions from eclipses, 37-42
Predictions through natal charts, 49-93
  careers, 54, 79-82
  children, 55-56, 69, 79, 84-85 (see also Predictions about children)
  compatibility, 82-87
  cultural factors, 5, 32
  environmental factors, 31-32
  friends and enemies, 85-87
  health, mental, 75-76; parental, 55-57; physical, 68-70
  love and attraction, 83-84

  marriage, 82-84
  travel, 87-88
Predictions using Primary Directions, 91-93
Prosperity (see Money and wealth)
Ptolemy's: achievements, *iii*, defense of astrology, 4-5; ancient scroll, 25-26; controversial lifespan formula, 64; outdated views, *iii-iv*
Quality of death, 88-89; planetary lords of, 88-89; planetary aspects, 89
Questions a natal chart can answer, 52-55
Reading natal charts, 49-89
  ascendant, 50-52
  basics, 6, 27-28
  dominant planet, figuring, 72
  dominant planets in, 72-75
  interpreting planetary aspects, 27-28, 52-55
  personality readings, 70-75
    basics, 70-72
    cultural factors, 5, 31
    environmental factors, 5, 31-32
    for infants, not recommended, 60, 61, 64
    health, 75-76
    houses, 53 (see also Twelve astrological houses)
    limitations of, 5, 6
    most important planets and factors, 50-51, 70-75
    planetary aspects in the chart, 70-75
      planetary placements in the chart, 10, 28, 54-55, 71-72
      in the quadrants, 10, 71, 75, 82, 87
    predictions (see Predictions)
    retrograde planets, meaning, 27-28
    ruling or governing planet of the chart, 54-55, 72-75
    and zodiac signs, 70-71
Relationships, 82-87
  friends and enemies, 85-87
  friendship indicators, 85-87
  love, attraction, and marriage, 82-84
  temporary, 86-87
Retrogrades, 11, 27-28; planetary stations, 11; 37-38, 54, 67, 71

Ruling planets of charts (see Reading natal charts)
Ruling planets of zodiac signs, 21
Sagittarius, 10, 13-14, 17, 19-21, 23-26, 32-34, 36, 40, 44, 57, 59, 62, 68-71, 75, 78, 81-82, 88-89
Sample questions and answers, 54-55
Saturn, 4, 9-15, 20-26, 33-35, 37, 41-42, 55-57, 59-60, 62-63, 65, 67-73, 75-76, 78-86, 88-90, 92
       natal Saturn, 56-57, 67-68, 72, 75, 78, 82, 84, 85, 86
Scorpio, 10, 13, 16-17, 19-26, 34-36, 40, 44, 57, 62, 66, 68-72, 81, 85-86, 88-89
Siblings, 35, 52-53, 57-58, 85
Seasons: resembling phases of life, 15; spring equinox, 15; and zodiac signs, 43-44; weather (see Weather)
'Sects', defined, 10
Seven Ages of Man, 90
Sextile, planetary aspect, defined, 18-19
Sextiles of:
       Sun, 56, 82
       Moon, 45, 56, 82
       Venus, 26, 56
       Mars, 65
       Saturn, 56, 65
Shooting stars (see Meteors)
Solar eclipses (see Eclipses)
'Solid' signs (today called 'fixed' signs) (see Zodiac signs)
Solstitial zodiac signs Cancer and Capricorn, 40, 43
Spaces between planets (see Orbs)
Square, planetary aspect, defined, 18-19
       Squares of:
       Sun, 56, 83, 87, 89, 92
       Moon, 56, 57, 70, 75, 82, 87, 89, 92
       Venus, 56-57
       Mars, 56, 60, 63, 65, 68, 87, 89
       Saturn, 56-57, 60, 63, 65, 68, 89
Sun, *iii*, 1, 3-5, 7-13, 15-17, 20-23, 25-27, 31-34, 36-38, 40-43, 45-46, 50-51, 54-63, 65, 67-70, 75-76, 78-80, 82-92
       adaptable quality, 9

natal Sun, 42, 54-58, 61, 63, 65, 67, 68, 75, 78, 82, 85, 87, 92
    neutralizing Anaretas, 63
Sun and Moon (see Planets)
Supplements to the natal chart, 90-91
Table of essential planetary dignities, 62
Table of planets in home signs, exaltation, and fall, 62
Table of planetary terms, Ptolemy's, 26
Table of planetary terms, traditional, 24
Table of zodiac signs of planetary exaltation and fall, 23
Taurus, 10, 12, 16-17, 19-26, 32-34, 36, 39-40, 43, 57, 62, 68-72, 81, 83, 88-89
'Terms,' subdivisions of zodiac signs, basics, 24-26; Table of, Ptolemy's, 26; Table of, traditional, 24 (see also Zodiac signs)
Tetrabiblos: meaning, *iii*; 'Paraphrase of Proclus', *iii*, *iv*, 93; table of contents, *vii-ix*; translations, *iii-iv*, 66
Time lords, planetary, 92
Transits, planetary, 7, 78, 86, 92
Travel, 87-88
Trine, planetary aspect, defined, 18-19, 27; in general, 5, 53, 54, 56, 82
    Trines of:
    Sun, 54, 56, 82
    Moon, 45, 56, 82
    Venus, 56, 83
    Mars, 65, 83
    Saturn, 56, 65
Triplicities (zodiac signs grouped as fire, earth, air, or water signs), 21-22
    of nations, 32-36
Twelve astrological 'houses' and their meanings, 53-55
    ancient epithets for, 62, 87
    basics, 19, 25, 53-54
    divided into 'terms', (see Terms)
Venus, 4, 9-15, 20-27, 33-36, 41-42, 55-57, 59, 62, 65, 67, 69-71, 73-76, 78-90, 92
    natal Venus, 55, 56, 65, 67, 70, 75, 78, 82, 84, 85, 86, 87
Virgo, 10, 12, 17, 19-26, 33-34, 36, 39-40, 44, 57, 59, 62, 68-69, 71, 75, 78, 81-82, 85, 88-89
Weather, forecasting, 42-47
Zenith, 8, 15, 52

Zodiac signs
- air, earth, fire, and water, 21-22
- animals in, 39, 59, 68, 88
- 'beholding' and 'mirroring', 20, 63
- 'bicorporeal', defined, 17; 71
- and body type, 68
- cardinal, 71
- cardinal, fixed, and mutable signs, 16-17, 71
- and careers, 81
- decans and the weather, 43
- disjunct, 20
- 'fertile' Cancer, Scorpio, and Pisces, 85
- fixed (also called 'solid'), 71, 88
- fixed stars in, 11-13
- four elements: air, earth, fire, water, 20-22
- 'masculine' and 'feminine', 17-18
- mutable (also called 'bicorporeal') signs, defined, 16, 71
- obsolete concepts
  - 'commanding' and 'obeying', 19
  - 'faces,' 'chariots' and 'thrones', 26-27
- and personality traits, 71
- ruling planets, 21
- ruling signs of nations, 36
- 'solstitial' and 'equinoctial', 16
- star clusters, 69
- 'terms' (subdivisions of zodiac signs), 24-26
- 'terrestrial' and 'aquatic' signs, 81
- triplicities ('fire, earth, air, water'), 21-22

Zodiac, what is, 15

www.ingramcontent.com/pod-product-compliance
Lightning Source LLC
Chambersburg PA
CBHW080639170426
43200CB00015B/2900